A Case of Modern Day Pharisees

The Need for Holiness

George E Pfautsch

authorHOUSE®

AuthorHouse™
1663 Liberty Drive
Bloomington, IN 47403
www.authorhouse.com
Phone: 1-800-839-8640

Published by AuthorHouse   2/15/2012

ISBN: 978-1-4685-4324-7 (sc)
ISBN: 978-1-4685-4323-0 (e)

Contents

Preface

There was a great deal of reluctance on my part to publish this book. My reluctance was due to the fact that it would be necessary for me to be critical of actions taken by some people for whom I have a great deal of respect. In my opinion, those people and their organizations were trying to apply social justice to a situation in a manner they believed was morally proper. My reluctance also resulted from the concern I have that some readers will read this book as another "slam" against the Catholic Church's methods used in dealing with sexual abuse cases.

Despite these concerns it is my belief that the purposes for writing this book transcend the reasons for not writing it. If everyone involved in this case had followed our Lord's message to be merciful, compassionate and loving, the moral conflicts involved could have been avoided. The major purpose of the book is to remind readers that the moral path He designed for us leads to peace and to a greater love of Him and of one another. Forgiveness, mercy, compassion and love was the message He was urging the Pharisees to follow. It is also the message He urges us to follow.

Another reason for publishing the book deals with my previous writings on the importance of following faith-based morality. In those writings I have placed morality into three categories; secular-based, religion-based and faith-based. They are very much involved in the story of this book. My writings have previously dealt with situations where secular-based morality came into conflict with faith-based morality. In this case it was religion-based morality that was applied in a manner which appears to have come into conflict with faith-based morality.

The above, then, are the reasons for proceeding with the book. It is a true story and one about which you, the reader, will form your own opinion of the "right" morality, based on your personal understandings of what He who made us would have done.

My references to faith-based morality are my attempts to describe morality as I believe our Lord defines it for us. As flawed human beings that is not always easy for us to do because our faith is individualistic and our understanding of His wishes is also somewhat individualistic. Even when we do our best to understand His wishes and His ways, we sometimes fail.

George E Pfautsch

Introduction

This book addresses a sad story. No matter how much can be said that may be of redeeming value, it will never be enough to restore a better life for hundreds and soon thousands of poor children in Honduras who have forever been deprived of a better life. It is being told to you in order that the causes of the needless harm done to those children may be avoided in the future. The moral lessons to be learned will be examined throughout this book.

It is my hope that this book will serve our Lord's purpose. If not, its purpose is meaningless.

It was sometime in the late 1980's or early 1990's that my wife and I became familiar with the work of Father Emil Cook. By that time, Father Emil had been in Honduras for about twenty years and had built several sites for poor boys and girls in Honduras. It seemed like the kind of mission we were interested in supporting.

Father Emil was very dedicated to the poor and was doing exceptionally good work for them, especially the youth. An acquaintance told me Father Emil was a man who had a small and somewhat disheveled office and would spend many hours communicating on an old typewriter with donors and prospective donors.

She also explained that Father Emil did not only believe in just providing food, shelter and education for the poor children, but also believed that they needed to be taught the basics of how to be self-sufficient and productive citizens. In the view of my wife and myself, the latter is an important aspect of helping the poor.

Father Emil also believed an education included helping the children increase their knowledge of and faith in God and therefore taught them the importance of growing their spiritual wisdom. Such training too, is an extremely important aspect of increasing one's overall knowledge and wisdom, and that training further impressed us.

Thereafter, my wife and I began contributing to the work of Father Emil via an organization located in Wisconsin, which is now named Mission Honduras International and sometimes referred to as just Mission Honduras or MHI. For many years thereafter, Father Emil would write us and other donors once or twice a year to inform us of the activities of his mission, and the expansions his mission was making to assist more and more boys and girls and also poor and abandoned women.

We considered Father Emil's work to be an outstanding model of what good missions in poor countries should be doing. Throughout the past twenty plus years we have maintained that view. As noted earlier, his work also made the love and understanding of God an important aspect of education.

Over the years, Father Emil expanded his missions and created an organization, APUFRAM, which is the Spanish acronym for the Association of Franciscan Boys' Towns and Girls' Towns. That organization was dedicated to carrying out the work and vision of Father Emil. Eventually the organization expanded into the Dominican Republic and Liberia, Africa.

Following their move into Africa, APUFRAM was providing assistance to more than 1,000 children annually in the three countries in which they operated. As Father Emil turned more and more of the mission work over to APUFRAM personnel, he began spending more of his time raising funds for the organization. He made yearly trips to the United States and frequently spent up to five months a year here on his fundraising efforts. He would often travel 25,000 miles or more by car during those trips.

Mission Honduras, which was the funding vehicle for Father Emil, moved from Milwaukee to Chicago. It was through Mission Honduras that most of the funds raised by Father Emil flowed. Funds would be transferred from Mission Honduras as needed to the APUFRAM organization.

By 2008, Mission Honduras International's revenues were exceeding well over a million dollars annually and the missions in Honduras, the Dominican Republic and Liberia were thriving and expanding. The primary work of these missions was helping many poor children in some of the poorest countries in the world.

The missions were staffed by members of APUFRAM. The members of APUFRAM were Hondurans who at one time had been recipients of aid in the earlier days of Father Emil's work.

These Honduran missionaries were now operating in foreign countries and with foreign cultures.

Having been helped themselves, it was an idealistic desire of APUFRAM personnel to, in turn, help others. That dream would also prove to have some nightmarish aspects.

In early July, 2009, we received a letter from Mission Honduras International that would change the entire mission work of Father Emil and APUFRAM for many years to come and very likely forever.

Through his forty years in Honduras, Father Emil has sacrificed much to aid the poor. He and APUFRAM have assisted almost 30,000 children during his forty years in Honduras. The letter received by us provided some fairly scant details that would turn the many sacrifices made by Father Emil into an even greater struggle.

The sequence of events before and after the July, 2009, letter have been of interest because my wife and I have been long time donors. The events were also of substantial interest to me as an author because of earlier writings on morality. We can put morality into three categories. Secular-based morality refers to the conduct determined by human laws and regulations and other actions which are not based on faith or religion. Such conduct may or may not incorporate faith-based morality. Faith-based morality derives from faith in God and the conduct that flows from obeying his commands and wishes. Religion-based morality incorporates the tenets of specific, denominational religions. Much of such morality is based on faith but also goes into the procedures, practices and rules of the religion involved.

All actions of humans fall into one of the above three categories. By placing the actions of humans into these three categories of morality we can better determine the justifications or lack thereof of actions taken by various people and organizations as they relate to Father Emil and APUFRAM, the organization founded by him.

A small portion of this book is about Father Emil Cook, a humble man dedicated to the work of our Creator. It is also about APUFRAM, an organization he founded. However most of the book is the story of how the events related to this case did great harm to the work of Father Emil and his organization in Honduras and how they may have violated the faith-based morality given to us by our Lord in the process. The actions taken in this case have greatly harmed some of the poorest of poor children in the world.

The harm caused by members of the Catholic hierarchy was no doubt unintended. They relied on standards and procedures in an attempt to provide justice. In this case the standards and procedures were applied in a manner that seem to have deviated from our Lord's teaching to be loving, kind, merciful and compassionate.

Chapter 1 --- Crusaders For The Poor

The life of Father Emil Cook began on September 30, 1939, in St. John's Hospital in Salina, Kansas. He was the first and only child of William Francis and Margaret Jane (O'Brien) Cook.

He was named William Francis Cook, Jr. but during his youth was nicknamed, "Buddy" or "Sonny".

Buddy was born at a time when the values of this nation were far different than today. It was still the period of the Great Depression and a time when war was beginning to rage in Europe and would soon include this nation. It was a time when important values included having shelter and food. It was not a period of excesses. It was a time when the appreciation of a simple life mattered much more to the citizens of this country. Those simple values learned during his youth would serve Buddy in good stead during his adult life.

Buddy grew up in rural America. The Cooks lived in a small, five-room home that was surrounded by ten acres of farmland and was located near the city of Salina. For many Americans of that era, life entailed a combination of work, when jobs were available, and some farm activities. During the day William Sr. worked in a feed mill and Margaret worked at the school cafeteria. The early morning hours and evening hours were spent on farm activities.

Compared to many people of that time, the Cooks, who lived a simple life, nevertheless lived a life that provided adequate shelter and food. Many others at that time who lived in the city, and had no job, were forced to rely on soup lines to keep body and soul together. The Cooks' modest jobs and income from farm activities were enough to provide them a typical life for that period of time. The people of that era, often needed to be and were resourceful people. Canning fruits and vegetables, making jelly and butter were common practices. That simple and resourceful early life would also stand Buddy in good stead through the remainder of his life.

By the time he was twelve years old, Buddy decided that he wished to be a priest. He also decided that he wanted to be a Franciscan priest and a missionary in Latin America. After he completed his school years in Salina, he entered the seminary of the Conventual Franciscans of Our Lady of Consolation in Mt. St. Francis, Indiana. He was ordained a priest in 1966 and became Father Emil Cook. Following his ordination he was assigned as an assistant pastor to the parish of Trinity Guadalupe in Milwaukee, Wisconsin. But his goal to become a missionary in Latin America remained.

In 1970, at the age of 30, Father Emil, left his comfortable surroundings in the United States and headed to Honduras to bring God to the poor. Soon he was also bringing food, shelter, and education to poor children. He also taught them the value of hard work. He started with one small simple school, but was determined to do more. He thought and dreamed about the day there would be an organization that could carry out and expand his vision and his mission.

It was in 1986 that Father Emil's dream became a reality. By then, those who had been through his school and had gone on to become university graduates formed APUFRAM. The organization, with the financial support obtained through Father Emil's fundraising efforts, grew steadily. Today, they operate a mission that includes a number of elementary and high schools, orphanages, boys and girls boarding schools, a trade school, university housing and a shelter for abandoned mothers and children.

APUFRAM also has farming operations that provide for about fifty percent of the support required to educate as many as 900 students in Honduras. These farming operations are also the method whereby the children work and thus provide for some of the necessities (food, clothing, maintenance and other necessities of daily life) for their education. The income from these farming operations would become critical as this sad story unfolds.

APUFRAM raises cattle which provide food. They raise chickens which also provide food via eggs and they sell eggs to provide much needed cash to maintain their facilities. They raise and sell bananas and African palms. Some use their skills in arts and crafts to raise funds. They are young farmers and entrepreneurs. All learn the value of hard work.

Father Emil is truly a crusader for the poor as are the members of APUFRAM. Their motto of God - Study - Work, says much about their aspirations for others as it did for themselves at one time. They understand that a strong belief in God is a necessary part of education. It is through that belief that human beings in their early years begin to better understand the importance of spiritual wisdom. Study is necessary for humans to create a better life for themselves and others in the time spent on earth. Work teaches students early in life of the sacrifices that are required to provide a better life in this world and the next.

Based on public information provided by the International Monetary Fund, Honduras was ranked as the third poorest country in the Americas in 2010. That ranking is based on Gross Domestic Product per capita. Only Haiti and Nicaragua were ranked as poorer nations. It is a rarity for poor children in Honduras to obtain more than a couple of years of education. Most are then forced to work in order to support their families. Much of the work, even at the ages of nine and ten consists of very physical labor.

For the poor children of Honduras, APUFRAM provides hundreds of them with hope. Hope for being rescued from a life of deprivation. Hope for an education and hope for a better life so they too can one day provide hope for others who are in the beginning years of a difficult life, as they once endured.

The story of APUFRAM can best be understood from those who have benefited from it. In his words, a former student, Denis Arturo Erazo, explains the role APUFRAM and Father Emil played in his life.

As a child, I was very happy living with my parents and grandparents, but unfortunately, I had very little time with them. They died when I was a young boy and from that point on my life took another direction. I went to live with some relatives who took advantage of me by sending me out to sell in the streets of Tegucigalpa at some risk to my life. It was at that time, that through contacts of an uncle, I enrolled with APUFRAM in 1994, along with my brothers Luis, Hector and Jairo. Jairo is the youngest of my brothers and is now in the early stages of his studies at the university.

In APUFRAM, I found not only family warmth but also the hope that I had lost and was able to go forward and become a better person with a better future. Now I have finished my studies in Agro-Industrial Engineering. During my time in the university I assisted in one of the boys-towns where I had spent much time - the St. Francis of Assisi Boys Town. There I worked as a house director during the mornings and in the afternoon I attended classes at the university.

I have learned to serve others and I feel happy because APUFRAM has helped me so much. I share the philosophy of Father Emil: "To serve others and to be able to help the many people who are in need". God bless the heart of Father Emil and his tireless efforts to serve and help the poor.

APUFRAM has made the differences for me and for many young people. They have transformed our lives so we can become successful and honorable people in our country.

Stories similar to Denis' are repeated time and time again by the students of APUFRAM. As he so appropriately stated it, they are transformed from a life of deprivation to one of success and with a love of their Creator. As noted earlier, in the twenty-five years it has been in existence, almost 30,000 children have been through their program. It is truly a beacon of light for many of the poor in Honduras.

APUFRAM has been and continues to be a supporter of the Catholic Church in Honduras. It has been a builder of many churches and has helped with repairing churches and it helps to financially support priests who serve in poor areas.

It pays the salaries of pastoral workers in remote rural areas of Honduras where priests cannot visit very often. For many rural children this is their only exposure to the teachings of the Church. Because of reduced funding, APUFRAM has had to reduce the number of pastoral workers it can support. On weekends Father Emil has been saying numerous Masses in rural areas where local people otherwise would not be able to attend Mass.

The members of APUFRAM wanted to be missionaries beyond Honduras. Their goal was to help others in poor countries just as they had been helped. They began a mission in the Dominican Republic and in the early part of the new millennium they crossed the Atlantic Ocean to open a mission in Liberia, Africa.

The mission in Liberia was to bring grief to the APUFRAM organization in early 2009. One of the missionaries they sent to Liberia was accused of and eventually confessed to having raped a young Liberian girl. As so often occurs, one charge led to other allegations against the organization's personnel in Honduras.

The "Case" noted in the title of this book began with the rape case in Liberia. However, this entire case was to continue for several years and is still ongoing. As this book is being written numerous aspects of this case remain unresolved. It is a case that pits one standard of morality against other standards of morality.

As noted earlier, in addition to being a donor to the mission in Honduras, this case became of great interest to me because of the moral issues involved. My early books were focused on the moral issues of our nation. This case, however, involved members of the same Church and resulted from viewing morality from different perspectives. When moral issues involve the bitterness that this case involved, it is worth reviewing the moral issues to see if there was a method of looking at the moral issues that could have negated most of the bitterness. Examining the moral issues will be the focus of the remainder of this book.

Chapter 2 ~~~ The Pharisees

The title of this book, "A Case of Modern Day Pharisees" was selected because, in my opinion, it best describes the moral actions taken by some in this case. As a reader you can and undoubtedly will form your own opinion.

So let us start by taking a look at some of the issues Jesus had with the Pharisees. Sometimes I think the Pharisees have been given a bum rap over the many years since Jesus lived on earth. Many Pharisees were people who, in all likelihood, were very sincere in their beliefs and laws which had been a part of their religion for many years. Before we castigate the Pharisees too much, it is also good to remember that St. Paul was a Pharisee as well as a great believer. Jesus even reminded his followers to observe their laws. Jesus had no problem with the laws of the Pharisees. It was their hypocritical use of the laws that frustrated and annoyed Him.

All of us at times play the role of the Pharisees, inasmuch as we violate the wishes of Jesus and hold to the belief that certain procedures must be observed without bringing love and mercy into our actions. When we perform in a manner that violates the wishes of Jesus we err. Jesus was God, and as God, He could not err and He has made his wishes known to us. If we could always follow His wishes our moral actions would be flawless.

The moral lessons Jesus was teaching when discussing the shortcomings of the Pharisees at that time in history also apply to us today. When we act in accord with the laws and standards we have today but do so without compassion, mercy and love, we too are guilty of being pharisaical.

It was those situations where the application of rules got in the way of spiritual wisdom, which Jesus disliked regarding the morality of the Pharisees. To see this difference we need to look at some examples when Jesus and the Pharisees differed.

In Chapter nine of Matthew, verses 9-13 we read, *As Jesus passed on from there he saw a man named Matthew sitting at the customs post. He said to him, "Follow me." And he got up and followed him. While he was at the table in his house many tax collectors and sinners came and sat with Jesus and his disciples. The Pharisees saw this and said to his disciples, "Why does your teacher eat with tax collectors and sinners?" He heard this and said, "Those who are well do not need a physician, but the sick do. Go and learn the meaning* of the words, 'I desire mercy, not sacrifice.' I did not come to call the righteous but sinners."

In the APUFRAM case there were far too many people who also did not heed the words of Jesus. The rape of a teenager in Liberia was certainly a serious offense but excessive righteousness became the word of the day as opposed to having mercy for those who sinned. The search to apply punishment was a problem in the case of APUFRAM. Mercy and love were frequently forgotten.

In Chapter twelve of Matthew, verses 9-14, Jesus again irritated the Pharisees with His compassion. *He left that place and went to the synagogue. A man with a shriveled hand happened to be there, and they put this question to Jesus, hoping to bring an accusation against him. "Is it lawful to work a cure on the Sabbath?" He said in response "Suppose one of you has a sheep and it falls into a pit on the Sabbath. Will he not take hold of it and pull it out? Well, think how much more precious a human being is than a sheep. Clearly good deeds may be performed on the Sabbath." To the man he said, "Stretch out your hand." He did so, and it was perfectly restored; it became as sound as the other. When the Pharisees were outside they began to plot against him to find a way to destroy him.*

Here again the Pharisees were spiritually blind in their narrow focus to observe the law of the Sabbath. They could not understand that Jesus' teaching was about understanding, love, compassion, and mercy.

When any of us become so immersed in laws, procedures and rules that we forget the teaching of Jesus and take actions that violate the teachings of Jesus we err morally. And we often do it without even knowing that we are doing it.

It was not the laws of the Pharisees that was the problem in the mind of Jesus. In fact in Matthew 23, Jesus emphasized that point, *Then Jesus told the crowds and his disciples. "The scribes and the Pharisees have succeeded Moses as teachers, therefore do everything they tell you. But do not follow their example. Their words are bold but their deeds are few."*

Those words described the problem Jesus had with the Pharisees. They were strict believers and observers of their laws, but at times they were spiritually blind. They could read the words but did not understand the spirit of the words. That is still a problem that is with us today and will be with us in the future, because we are sinners.

It is well for all of us to always remember the words that conclude the Prologue of the Catechism of the Catholic Church, "The whole concern of doctrine and its teaching must be directed to the love that never ends. Whether something is proposed for belief, for hope or for action, the love of our Lord must always be made accessible, so that anyone can see that all the works of perfect Christian virtue spring from love and have no other objective than to arrive at love."

There was a certain degree of spiritual blindness in the case involving APUFRAM and there was most assuredly a lack of love. Most of the strife in this case was due to those factors.

One thing Jesus made clear during his time on earth was the care all of us should have for the poor. In the Sermon on the Mount and in many other situations he mandated compassion for the poor.

Of the two major moral issues that are involved in the case of APUFRAM one can be found in the Church's standards and procedures on dealing with clerical sexual abuse, but more importantly, the second issue concerns the teachings Jesus gave us regarding the poor. If both had been applied with the spiritual wisdom Jesus sought from all of us there would have been no problems.

The standards that have been put in place in recent years regarding sexual clerical abuse are important and very much needed. These standards and procedures at this time in the Church are a very high profile issue because of the many cases that have surfaced over the past few years. In this case, the excessive attention to those procedures seemed to result in dismissing Jesus' desire that we help the poor.

Before disclosing all the other moral issues that have taken place in this case it is best to first explore the events that occurred. Due to the confidential nature of charges brought against a few people of APUFRAM some of the facts of this case remain unknown to the public, but there are facts that are known and these facts will be examined. It may be that some of the facts that are unknown have contributed to some of the questionable decisions that were made. When the issues arise that involve faith-based morality and the decisions seem dubious, they will be noted. No decisions that were made which violate the wishes of our Lord can be justified.

Many readers will no doubt believe the analogy with the Pharisees to be somewhat unfair, but inasmuch as some parties still subordinate the priority of Jesus' teaching regarding the poor to the procedures involving clerical abuse, that analogy will be made when this writer believes it is deserved.

At times my own actions in this case were pharisaical. Too often, my pleadings to not deprive the poor Honduran children of a better life went beyond pleadings. Sometimes we fail. All of us need his mercy and we need to be contrite when we err.

Chapter 3 --- The Tragic Events Of 2009

*M*y knowledge of APUFRAM and their personnel was very limited prior to 2009. That limited knowledge also applied to Mission Honduras International. In the latter case my impression was that it was primarily a P O Box to which I submitted contributions and which were then transferred to Honduras for the use of Father Emil's missions. I did recall occasionally receiving a newsletter and that there was a letter regarding an expansion into Liberia. Our only regular contact was with Father Emil. That would change in 2009.

In early July, 2009, we received a letter from the Acting President of the Board of Directors of Mission Honduras International (MHI). I do not recall ever having received any prior correspondence from him. The letter noted that the Board had become aware of a sexual abuse incident committed by one of the Honduran managers in Liberia against a teenage Liberian girl. It also indicated that some other allegations had been brought to the attention of the Board.

The part of the letter that drew most of my attention was the Board's decision to suspend funding to APUFRAM until certain "corrective policies, procedures, and programs" were in place and implemented. Somehow that seemed contrary to the teachings of Jesus to help the poor and also seemed somewhat self-destructive.

My immediate thoughts were that it was an error to suspend funding as a first step. I assumed there were many donors such as myself who were contributing due primarily to the efforts of Father Emil and for the support of his missions in Honduras and the Dominican Republic. I was not very familiar with the operation in Liberia.

Shortly thereafter I sent an e-mail of my concerns to the Acting President of the MHI Board in regards to the restriction on funding. I also asked him to share my e-mail with the other Board members. I noted that it had always been the intention of my wife and myself to donate to the operations in Honduras and that we wanted to be assured that the funds we had contributed were going to be donated to the Honduran missions.

As a result of my communications two events occurred. One was a response from the Executive Director of MHI that assured me that my contributions did go to Honduras. It was the first and only time that I received an e-mail from her. Although I did not save the e-mail, I recall it very well and remember it being a very short e-mail which said that the funds I contributed were a part of the $600,000 that Father Emil took with him to Honduras. That e-mail would be remembered by me later for different reasons.

The other event was that I received another response from a member of the Board, named Joan Pharr. Her e-mail stated that she agreed with my concerns and that she had cast a dissenting vote on the decision to suspend funding. She subsequently was removed from the Board, for what seems to have been the casting of several dissenting votes and for being in disagreement with the other members of the Board.

My wife and I were concerned primarily that the suspension of funding would harm the poor children of Honduras. Although the MHI correspondence indicated that APUFRAM had cash reserves, it was not possible to ascertain if those were for emergency purposes or were reserves that were available for operations. In subsequent communications Father Emil indicated those reserves were indeed for emergencies and, if used, could be the demise of APUFRAM. As events developed his views on that have proven to be partially true.

We wished to continue helping the children of APUFRAM , but had no vehicle through which to do that. As things developed, Joan Pharr advised me that a small group of people were establishing an organization which was being formed to help fund APUFRAM. It was named APUFRAM International but had not as yet obtained tax-exempt status. They advised us that we could make tax deductible contributions through an organization named Special Missions Foundation.

As we were preparing to make a contribution, we received more correspondence from a Board member of MHI which stated that Special Missions Foundation would not accept donations on behalf of APUFRAM, once they were made aware of the sexual abuse situation. I called Special Missions Foundation and they advised me that MHI had misinformed me, and that they were indeed accepting donations that could be forwarded to APUFRAM. It did surprise me that the MHI Board seemed intent on cutting off every avenue of possible funding help to APUFRAM.

The issue of cutting off funding would surface a number of times.

As things proceeded into the fall of 2009 there were some indications that peace among the various parties could occur. A couple of meetings were scheduled between the various parties, which now included Mission Honduras International, APUFRAM, APUFRAM International, Special Missions Foundation, the Conventual Franciscans of the Orders in Indiana and Honduras and Father Emil. Through e-mails and various sources I was kept somewhat abreast of the meetings.

The meetings between these parties were held in October and November. There are different perceptions of the meetings. But a key part of the MHI letter to supporters which was mailed on December 1, 2009, stated the following in regards to the meeting of November 17 and 18:

APUFRAM agreed to two key elements discussed at length during the meeting: 1)to participate in the investigation of past allegations of child abuse within APUFRAM, and 2) to use the Child Protection Policy developed at the meeting in October as the base document for developing a new Child Protection Policy for APUFRAM.

By the date of the above-mentioned letter I had become familiar with the members of the MHI Board of Directors, two of the people who were establishing APUFRAM International, the Treasurer of Special Missions Foundation, and the Provincial of the Conventual Franciscans of Our Lady of Consolation who are based in Indiana. Father Emil had been familiar to me for many years although I have never met him. I also have never met anyone in the APUFRAM organization.

The above is noted because it was a goal of mine to promote peace among the parties and I had sent numerous e-mails to all of them imploring them to do that. My wife and I also wanted to continue supporting the poor children of APUFRAM. We believed it was a model program of how a good mission was to be operated, but we did not have any basis to believe or deny the allegations of sexual abuse within the organization. Also, my previous work on the books I had written regarding morality made this case of special interest to me.

It was my contention then and it is my contention now that the parties never made enough of an effort to understand each other or to seek an accord.

But with the letter that MHI had written to supporters, along with input from the people at APUFRAM International and Special Mission Foundation there was hope in the early part of December, 2009 that an accord, if not improved personal relations, could be achieved. One of the people with whom I had corresponded considerably up to that time was the Provincial of the Conventual Franciscans. My e-mails generally dwelled on the importance for him to consider the need of funding for the poor children of Honduras. He generally responded that their protection was his primary concern. I believed both goals could be accomplished simultaneously.

Those hopes were dashed on December 20, 2009, when the Provincial of the Conventual Franciscans sent me an e-mail. With the exception of the last paragraph, which was a personal response to some comments I had made earlier, that e-mail is reproduced below:

Sorry it's taken me a few days to respond to you. I was in Central America last week and was out of town yesterday.

Later today, I hope to have the final text of a letter that relays the results of our meeting in Central America involving Fr. Emil and the Definitories (boards) of the C.A. and the U.S. jurisdictions. I will send it to you.

Quite simply, the more information we receive the more concern we have about APUFRAM. There are things that have been done or not done that have pushed this to the brink. I share your concern for the ministry and children, but see how feet-dragging and denial on APUFRAM's part have continued to put the entire ministry at risk. (Not to mention how they seemingly walked away from 237 children in Liberia.) I am not sure what to say about helping to fund these ministries at present. MHI is trying to take care of Liberia, and I understand that the Diocese of Orlando has missions in the Dominican Republic. There is still a glimmer of hope that within a few months this will all be straightened out, but a lot of damage would have been done by then.

In the meantime, we have been compelled to notify the U.S. Bishops that Fr. Emil does not have permission to fund raise here in the U.S. With that prohibition, no one may use his name, image or likeness to fund raise as well. (This has been in force since mid-August but was recently violated.)

I know that both you and MHI have begun processes that could lead to legal action. I understand the reasons and emotions that underlie this. I do feel, however, that in the long run this will only hurt these ministries all the more.

As this book unfolds various parts of the above e-mail will be analyzed but I wish to immediately state that the provincial was in error regarding my intents in the final paragraph.

It was never my intent to start any legal proceedings. However, it was true that I had indicated my view that I thought the Attorney Generals within the States that had jurisdiction, if contacted, might be helpful in resolving certain issues.

The e-mail again seemed to place too much focus on the money aspects of the case. That view seemed to be saying that somehow behavior could be changed by cutting off the money supply.

The e-mail also seemed strange inasmuch as the Provincial seemed to believe he had the authority to tell everyone, including secular individuals and secular organizations that somehow they were duty bound by a Religious Order not to fund raise for APUFRAM. To this day that seems to have been an extraordinary and unusual effort to stifle fundraising by APUFRAM, APUFRAM International, Special Missions Foundation and others, which I believe went beyond his authority and touched on issues regarding the separation of church and state.

With that e-mail my hopes for reconciliation among the parties were dashed. My hope that a Provincial from the Franciscans, whose founder was one of the greatest advocates of peace, would eventually do all he could to pursue a path of peace was also dashed.

The Provincial was true to his word. In a letter to supporters of Mission Honduras International he sent the letter referred to in the e-mail he sent me. Many of the same points were made. He added the following specifics:

The MMP Definitory (Honduran Franciscan Board) *proposed and both Definitories unanimously agreed to the following measures.*

1 - Letter of obedience that Fr. Emil is to report to Saint Joseph Cupertino Friary of Comayaguela (Tegucigalpa) by 1 February 2010 to be involved in the ministry of the friars in the parish and is to cut himself off from the APUFRAM.

2- Put in place the safe environment policies as agreed to in October at Mount St. Francis, Indiana.

3 - Accept the conclusions of the truth commission investigation, led by Fr. John Stowe (who is friar of the

OLC province), a friar of the custody in Central America, and four Honduran professionals named by the custody.

4 - Fr. Emil is forbidden in any way to preach or raise funds for APUFRAM: the bishops of the U.S. should immediately be notified of this.

5- The above are to be applied until the results of a truth commission recommend otherwise.

That letter would motivate a greater action on my part for the following reasons:

1 - It seemed that the concern for the poor children of Honduras was related solely to their protection and not to their needs to obtain an overall better life.

2 - It seemed that a religious order in the United States was bypassing the justice system of the United States by attempting to dictate to secular people and organizations and also by dictating to a secular, foreign organization.

3 - It seemed that blocking funds to support the children in Honduras was an overriding factor.

4 - It seemed that a religious order in the United States was attempting to be the prosecutor, judge and jury for the affairs of foreign citizens and was circumventing the justice system of Honduras as well as this country.

The Provincial also followed through on his promise to notify the United States Bishops of the actions taken by the Conventual Franciscans. On December 22, 2009 on the letterhead of the United States Conference of Catholic Bishops the following Memorandum was released to all Bishops within the United States.

To: All Bishops

From: Msgr. Ronny Jenkins

Date: December, 22, 2009

Subject: **FR. EMIL COOK, AND "APUFRAM"**

The Office of the Minister Provincial of the Conventual Franciscan Friars has asked that the bishops of the United States be advised of the situation of Fr. Emil Cook, OFM Conv., and the ministries he is related to which operate under the organizational names "APUFRAM" ("Asociacion Pueblo Franciscan de Muchachos y Muchashas") and its fundraising arm, APUFRAM International.

APUFRAM has not demonstrated, to the Minister Provincial's satisfaction, that adequate safe environment programs have been enforced at locations it operates. As a result, Fr. Cook's Major Superior has denied him permission to raise funds in the United States. Thus, the Conventual Franciscans Friars do not endorse any fundraising whatsoever in the United States by APUFRAM, Fr. Cook or APUFRAM International.

25

If further information is needed, contact may be made with the Office of the Very Rev. James D. Kent, OFM Conv. Vicar and Acting Provincial, at 812-923-8444.

As this is being written, the following can be said:

1. Neither Father Emil Cook nor any other priest has been accused of sexual misconduct, which is now more than two years after the above was written and circulated.

2. APUFRAM was and is a secular, foreign organization operating under the laws of Honduras and to my knowledge no allegations of wrongdoing have been turned over to that country. No investigation has ever taken place.

3. APUFRAM International was only in the formational stages at the time the above was written and their only purpose was to help the poor and underprivileged children of Honduras obtain a better life. It seemed odd that they would be restricted in fund raising.

It seemed that the teaching of Jesus regarding the poor was not a significant consideration of the Conventual Franciscans. It also seemed that the USCCB staff either did not do its homework before circulating the above Memorandum or participated in the same decision as the Franciscans. Inasmuch as the USCCB has been in the forefront to help the poor in many countries it seems strange that in this case they discourage such help.

It was at Christmas-time in 2009 that the thought hit me that we have modern day Pharisees. That word also was used by a new acquaintance of mine who had become involved in the case. But there were still many facts that were missing, although there was no doubt that the poor children of Honduras were being harmed. It seemed that some in the Church hierarchy had become so concerned with the standards and procedures regarding clerical sexual misconduct that they too became spiritually blinded as did the Pharisees. Those standards and procedures are extremely important, but must never be administered in a way that harm the poor and would also provoke our Lord.

Chapter 4 --- The Moral Issues Regarding The Apufram Case

Throughout the Christmas Season of 2009, the funding restrictions that were circulated to the Bishops by the United States Conference of Catholic Bishops (USCCB) concerned me. I kept wondering how many of the facts of the case were familiar to the staff of the USCCB, who were responsible for circulating the memo of December 22, 2009. Even though I too was unfamiliar with many aspects of the case I decided to write the USCCB and ask that they review the case.

My letter dated January 2, 2010 set forth the facts as best I knew them at that time and were submitted to the USCCB. I wanted to also identify the moral issues that were involved. The letter is rather lengthy but contains my concerns at that point in time. It follows:

United States Conference of Catholic Bishops
Secretariat of Child & Youth Protection
3211 - 4th Street N E
Washington, D.C., 20017-1194

Recently, I became aware of a situation that involves the charge of a sexual abuse of a child in a foreign country (Liberia). The ramifications of the case are very complex and pit one good moral cause against another moral cause.

My interest in the case is as a long-time donor to the organization of the whistleblower, and my concerns that relate to the important moral issues, other than child protection. Also, I am not sure civil authorities of all nations involved have been notified of the allegations. Finally, I am an author of several books on faith and morals and this case, because it involves conflicting moral issues, may prompt future writings.

Before giving some very brief information on the case, let me enumerate at least a few of the moral issues:

1 - Child protection

2 - The negative effect of funding restrictions on poor children in Honduras and the Dominican Republic

3 - The negative effect of reduced funding for the poor children of Liberia

4 - The serious dissension caused by the conflicting but well intentioned interest of various parties in the moral issues

The various parties involved include the following:

1 - Father Emil Cook, a member of the Conventual Franciscan Order and the founder of missions in Honduras, the Dominican Republic and Liberia. He is also the primary fundraiser for the missions. Most, if not all people involved would probably agree his missions are of a saintly nature and in some ways parallel those of Mother Teresa. He is now under investigation and maybe only for association with workers who operate the missions in the three countries. He and his work have been known to me for many years. I knew none of the other people involved until after the allegations became public. He is one of the subjects of the investigations for reasons I do not know.

2 - APUFRAM - The Spanish acronym for the group founded by Father Emil to operate the missions in the various countries. They are now under investigation.

3 - Mission Honduras International (MHI) - The US funding arm for the missions and whistleblower. It has served as Father Emil's primary funding source for many years and to which I believe most of the funds he raised were initially deposited. Their fundraising efforts for the poor have been harmed due to their whistle blowing.

4 - APUFRAM International - Another funding arm for the missions, which is attempting to fill the funding gap caused by the MHI restriction on funding. They are now under funding restrictions and the subject of legal action by MHI.

5 - Special Missions Foundation - An involved funding party and also under funding restrictions. They too have been the subject of legal threats by MHI.

6 - Conventual Franciscan Order - They are located in Mount St. Francis, Indiana and have a related Order in Honduras. They are the administrator and investigator of the allegations. As noted earlier I don't know if they have notified civil authorities or if civil authorities have been involved.

Brief facts:

Because of confidentiality surrounding the case my information is very limited. In early 2009, MHI was made aware of an alleged sexual abuse to an alleged child in Liberia by a member of APUFRAM who had been sent to Liberia as the senior manager. The accused individual was jailed in Liberia but released shortly thereafter. Between that time and now, MHI's Board of Directors suspended funding to APUFRAM and I believe it was they who notified the Franciscan Conventual Fathers.

It is my understanding that additional abuse cases are alleged against APUFRAM. As noted above APUFRAM International has tried to fill the financial gap caused by the MHI funding restrictions. Subsequent fundraising restrictions imposed by the administrator and investigator on Father Emil, APUFRAM, and APUFRAM International have in turn brought Special Missions Foundation into the picture and they have acted as a conduit for transferring funds to APUFRAM.

Current situation and issues:

- Due to the allegations against APUFRAM, Father Emil has been subjected to Obedience by his Order and within a few weeks must divorce himself from APUFRAM activities. This creates an issue in my mind. Should he be held responsible for allegations against others? If that is logical must the Provincial of an Order also be responsible for every person accused of wrongdoing in his Order? If so, this would seem to say a pastor must be responsible for the moral conduct of his parishioners.

- Father Emil has also been restricted from any fundraising activities (which had been for the benefit of MHI until the incident occurred) along with other funding organizations who wish to assist APUFRAM in maintaining aid to poor children in Honduras and the Dominican Republic.

Consequently, APUFRAM has had to cut back its operations. The fundraising restriction seems onerous and a violation of our Lord's demand to help the poor. ARE SUCH ABSOLUTE FUNDING RESTRICTIONS APPROPRIATE IN THIS SITUATION WHERE IT IS THE POOR CHILDREN WHO ARE BEING HARMED? (note - caps added for emphasis)

- Due to their whistle blowing effort MHI has been forced to take over management of the Liberian mission, because

the alleged perpetrator was from APUFRAM. This has placed financial operating burdens on MHI. One source has informed me that their revenues have been significantly reduced and that may be harmful to the children in Liberia.

– The Conventual Franciscan Order has not placed any restrictions on fundraising by MHI which had been associated with Father Emil and have written a letter supporting fundraising for MHI, which may be proper but have simultaneously restricted any fundraising on behalf of APUFRAM by Father Emil, APUFRAM, APUFRAM International and possibly Special Missions Foundation, which does not appear proper. AGAIN, IS IT APPROPRIATE TO STIFLE ALL FUNDING FOR THE POOR IN TWO COUNTRIES? (note - caps added for emphasis)

– It has been brought to my attention that MHI has brought legal actions against members of APUFRAM International and threatened legal action against Special Missions Foundation regarding donor lists.

It is my belief that all parties are doing what they believe to be morally correct, but in the process prohibit other good moral actions. The greatest of these moral wrongs is to knowingly and willfully stifle funding which clearly has the effect of reducing support for the poor. It has also caused great dissension between various parties.

It may be that the standards of the USCCB on child protection force unintended harm and immoral actions in other areas. It may also be that the standards have not been applied as they should be even though well intentioned. It is my opinion that the prevention of abuse to children is important and I also believe that helping poor children is important. It should be left to our good Lord to decide which is more important. It seems he would want us to achieve both goals. Any standards restricting that should be reviewed and guidance provided for this case and others which may cause a conflict in good moral issues.

In any event I am requesting that the USCCB investigate this case so similar situations will not result in bringing about the moral damage to the poor as is being done in this case. This involves more than 1,000 children being helped every year by these organizations. I wonder if the good Lord would approve of disallowing help to hundreds and maybe thousands of children while allegations are being investigated? This seems to violate not only the teaching of our Catholic Church but also the teaching of our LORD.

I am sorry that more detailed information is not provided but the investigation is confidential. As noted at the outset, this is a very complex case.

Having reviewed that letter again as I write this chapter, I probably should have stated that our Lord was abundantly clear about his desire for all of us to help the poor, but did not have anything to say about the sexual abuse treatment of clergy. In retrospect, it was not necessary to restrict funding for the poor while also complying with the standards of procedures and rules relating to sexual abuse.

On January 10, 2010 the Executive Director of the Child and Youth Protection's office of the USCCB responded as follows:

Dear Mr. Pfautsch

I have received your letter asking that the USCCB investigate a situation involving Fr. Emil Cook and APUFRAM. Thank you for caring about the funding for the poor and Fr. Emil.

The mandate of the USCCB's Secretariat of Child and Youth Protection is to address the issue of clergy sexual abuse within the U.S. Catholic Church, and this issue falls outside that purview. However, I have forwarded your letter to Mr. Johnny Young, Executive Director of the USCCB's Secretariat of Migration and Refugee Services. I am not sure what authority or knowledge his Secretariat would have regarding this matter, but I asked that he review your letter.

Thank you for caring about the poor and about children.

When I received the above letter it appeared that the Executive Director seemed to have no knowledge of the USCCB memo that was distributed to Bishops the month before. However, I also did not make mention of the memo in my letter to her. Subsequently she confirmed to me that she was not aware of this case until she heard from me. That would be at odds with what the Provincial of the Conventual Franciscans would tell me later. He stated he sent his letter to the Secretariat of the Child and Youth Protection. It may be that the memo was handled so routinely that it simply did not draw much attention by anyone within the USCCB and was circulated without little if any review.

I was not surprised that the letter from the Executive Director stated this case was beyond the purview of the USCCB. That in turn made me wonder why it was within their purview to issue the memo and also why it was in the purview of the Conventual Franciscans to involve themselves so deeply in the case. It may be that they did not realize that APUFRAM , although a supporter of the Catholic Church, was a secular, foreign organization. Nevertheless, they should have known and they should also have alerted Honduran authorities of the allegations. To this date, I do not know if Honduran authorities have been informed or if the allegations have been disclosed to any others.

After having received the letter from the Executive Director of the USCCB Secretariat of Child and Youth Protection, my belief was strengthened that some of the actions of MHI and the Conventual

Franciscans were flawed both morally and legally; morally because the funding restrictions did violate the morality taught us by Jesus as relates to caring for the poor and legally because they circumvented the justice systems that should have been involved and that they decided to take judicial matters into their own hands.

For those reasons this case became more bothersome to me. After looking into more aspects of the situation I decided to write an article regarding my views. Rather than paraphrase its contents, the full text of the article follows:

QUESTIONABLE APPLICATIONS OF BISHOPS' STANDARDS HARMING POOR

In light of numerous cases, it is understandable that the United States Conference of Catholic Bishops (USCCB) would insist on stringent standards to provide protection against the abuse of minors. But sometimes a questionable application of standards can have unintended harmful effects. That is the situation in a case that is now harming the poor, especially children, in Honduras and the Dominican Republic.

Forty years ago a humble missionary, Father Emil Cook, went to Honduras. As he saw firsthand the terrible conditions of the poor, especially children, he became a one person crusader to do something. During the forty years he formed an organization, APUFRAM to carry out his vision of aiding others. APUFRAM (Spanish acronym for Association of Franciscan Boys Towns and Girls Towns) would operate not only in Honduras but also the Dominican Republic and Liberia. The APUFRAM organization, comprised of people who had once been helped by Father Emil, became a missionary organization to help others around the world.

In early 2009, the good work of APUFRAM was jolted by the news of an alleged sexual abuse of a young girl in Liberia by one of the APUFRAM lay missionaries from Honduras. The incident was reported to Mission Honduras International(MHI), the US funding arm for APUFRAM. MHI suspended funding for APUFRAM and reported the incident to the Conventual Franciscan Order in the United States. Father Emil, who had made annual fundraising trips to the United States is a member of this Order.

By late 2009, because of additional alleged abuse cases made by MHI, the Conventual Franciscan Order decided to launch an investigation. Consequently, in attempting to comply with their own rules and the Bishops standards on child protection, the US Franciscans have advised all US Bishops that fundraising activities by Father Emil, APUFRAM and APUFRAM International (a new US group formed to provide financial support), both of which are secular organizations, were not acceptable in the United States. In addition, Father Emil was ordered to cut his ties with APUFRAM, while the investigation is ongoing, even though he is not accused of any personal sexual abuse. Father Emil claims, that other than the case in Liberia, which has been investigated and now made public, he has never been aware of any cases of child abuse within the APUFRAM organization.

In October, 2009, in a joint letter distributed by MHI and APUFRAM, Father Emil apologized for any errors he and the APUFRAM Board made in the handling of the abuse case in Liberia, and in early 2010 the APUFRAM organization implemented a new and improved child protection plan. But, to date the restrictions on funding have not been removed and the investigation in Honduras has not begun.

It is difficult to ever justify the denial of funding for the poor when we consider the faith-based moral mandate to do that as given to us by our Lord. Representatives of MHI and the US Franciscans have declined to comment on why they oppose funding to aid poor children of Honduras and the Dominican Republic.

Because the investigation can require lengthy periods, the lack of fundraising efforts in the United States has already resulted in hundreds and could result in thousands of children in the poorest countries in the world being deprived of food, shelter, and education. Even the best of well intended procedures can have devastating effects in some circumstances.

In early January, 2010, the USCCB was asked to review this case. In their response the Secretariat of Child and Youth Protection noted, "The mandate of the USCCB's Secretariat of Child and Youth Protection is to address the issue of clergy sexual abuse within the U.S. Catholic Church, and this issue falls outside that purview". In addition to the dubious restriction on funding, this response raises the issue as to the degree, if any, religious orders domiciled in the United States should be involved when sexual abuses occur in foreign countries, which are operated by secular foreign-based missionary organizations even though they may be funded wholly or partially by US charitable organizations.

The above article was sent to many Bishops who headed dioceses in areas where Father Emil often made fundraising appearances. Sometime later the article was published in the "Catholic Voice" a diocesan newspaper.

At this point, which is almost two years after the above article was written, not much has changed. I have repeatedly asked the question, "Why does this case justify harming the poor?" I have never received an answer to that question. It is now more than two years since the restriction on funding memo was circulated by the USCCB, but at this point no investigation has begun, nor have allegations been submitted to others to do the investigation.

The overriding moral issue is the restriction on funding. The reasons for that are alluded to in the above article and will be reviewed at greater length in the next chapter.

Chapter 5 --- Defining Morality And Acting Accordingly

When writing a book such as this one, it is important to keep in mind the beginning words of Chapter 7 from the gospel of Matthew.

Stop judging that you may not be judged. For as you judge, so will you be judged, and the measure with which you measure will be measured out to you. Why do you notice the splinter in your brother's eye, but do not perceive the wooden beam in your own eye? How can you say to your brother, 'Let me remove that splinter from your eye,' while the wooden beam is in your eye? You hypocrite, remove the wooden beam from your eye first: then you will see clearly to remove the splinter from your brother's eye.

I pray that the Holy Spirit gives me the wisdom to remember those words as I write the remainder of this book.

Life on earth has been described as a spiritual warfare and that it is. All human beings are spiritually flawed creatures and the stain of original sin is with us throughout this life. In his letter to the Galatians Saint Paul aptly described the evils of the flesh. But he also told us that, "the fruits of the spirit (or our soul) are love, joy, peace, patience, kindness, generosity, faithfulness, gentleness and self-control". Those traits were too often lacking in this case.

Saint Paul described the spiritual warfare in Chapter 7 of his letter to the Romans. "What I do, I do not understand. For I do not do what I want, but I do what I hate". Life is truly a spiritual warfare. It is our purpose in life to better know Him who created us. Through a greater understanding of Him who created us and the messages He gave us, we are better able to love Him and serve Him. But no matter how hard we try, we fail, as St. Paul indicated. It is only through his mercy that we are saved. Nevertheless, we must try to let our soul dictate our actions as best we are able to do that. That results in the best morality we can achieve. It is the Holy Spirit who dwells within our soul when we are in a state of grace.

In the early books I have written, attempts were made by me to place all moral actions of human beings into three categories. Later in this chapter those categories will be defined at greater length but first let me again provide you with an article that was written recently by me and will hopefully give you a greater insight into the reasons the restrictions on funding in the APUFRAM situation are morally unacceptable. The article follows:

FATHER EMIL AND APUFRAM - THE MORAL DECISIONS

Throughout our daily life we make moral decisions, all of which fall into three categories – 1) secular-based morality 2) religion-based morality and 3) faith-based morality.

Secular-based morality has no specific foundation upon which actions are based. For example, the laws of our nation are based on secular decisions. They may or may not be religion or faith-based. As cultures change, secular-based morality also tends to change.

Religion-based morality is based on religious beliefs and may include procedures and rules, as well, which are not faith-based. Within the Catholic Church most religion-based morality is faith-based morality but often goes beyond. Thus, Catholic and other religions have rules and procedures that are not based on faith alone. For example, Catholic practices are different than Muslim practices. The Catholic Church's procedures and rules covering sexual clerical abuse are also secular inasmuch as they are not based on the teachings of Jesus.

Faith-based morality is based on the teaching of Jesus Christ. It ALWAYS provides the best moral decisions and should supersede any other moral decision when moral decisions may be in conflict. It is based on the two commandments Jesus gave us and on other moral messages He has provided.

When any of us are confronted with a moral decision, and if that moral decision can be founded in the teachings of Christ, then we can be assured it is the proper moral decision.

The decisions in the case of Father Emil and APUFRAM involved both religion-based and faith-based morality. The decisions of Mission Honduras International, the Conventual Franciscans and the United States Conference of Catholic Bishops involved the faith-based issue of helping the poor and also the procedures of the Church regarding clerical sexual abuse (religion-based).

Jesus DID give us instructions regarding the poor but He did NOT give us guidance regarding clerical sexual abuse.

All three organizations seem to have erred morally inasmuch as they permitted a religion-based procedure to override the faith-based moral mandates of Jesus to help the poor. They had other options available to them regarding the manner in which they chose to correct the situation, (assuming a correction was necessary), but all chose to use an option which appears to have violated Jesus' teaching to aid the poor in Honduras.

In making the decision they chose to put secular Church rules regarding clerical sexual abuse ahead of the teaching of Christ. Demanding that the teaching of Christ be put aside when making any decision can never be a proper moral decision.

The categories of secular, religion and faith-based morality merit some additional explanations.

Secular-based morality is the most common form of morality for most of us. Our daily lives involve many forms of activity that we perform in a secular manner. Neither religion nor faith generally dictate the way we perform many of our daily chores. Neither the Bible nor Church teaching tell the mother how to cook a meal or dress her children. They do not tell the mill worker how to perform his or her job. Our daily activities are based on the way secular job descriptions and secular directions dictate. Secular laws also influence how fast we may drive. Even though most of our daily moral actions are secular they can be performed in a way that is based on faith. For example a mill worker's actions are based on secular rules but if he/she does something willfully that harms a fellow worker then that person violates faith-based morality.

At times however, secular laws come into conflict with faith-based morality. That was true of slavery and today is true of the sanctity of life. All of us need to remember that secular-based morality has no foundation of specific beliefs as do religion and faith-based morality. Secular based morality often depends on the mores and laws of secular societies.

Religion-based morality is often based on faith. The intent of religions is to follow a creed that best complies with the laws of God or Muhammad or Buddha or whatever is the foundation of beliefs of the particular religion. But religions often have procedures and rules that they believe help followers of the religion better comply with their particular belief system. As noted earlier in this book, Jesus had no problem with the rules of the Pharisees. He had a problem with the fact that they did not carry out their rules in a spiritual manner.

Faith-based morality is based on the teachings of Jesus. His two commandments and his teachings are the foundation of such morality. But even when one may know his wishes perfectly, which is doubtful, there is still the need to carry out his wishes as He would have us act. Therein is a great problem for all of us, because we are all sinners. Most of us have a pretty good understanding of what may be morally right in the eyes of Jesus but doing what is morally right becomes the problem. That is why we need his mercy. When we know and do what he wants us to do then we think and act in a faith-based moral manner.

In the case of Father Emil and APUFRAM, there is probably nothing wrong with the standards, procedures and rules that the Church has relating to child protection. However, they are more secular in nature than they are in faith. They also continue to evolve as just happened a few months prior to this writing. At a Bishops conference in Seattle the Charter regarding child protection was amended. That is the nature of secular rules. On the other hand the wishes of Jesus have remained constant. He is God and He is divine. Therefore what he has stated to be proper morality cannot and will not change. The danger of rules in this case occurred when the application of such rules conflicted with the wishes of Jesus as relates to the poor.

The procedures themselves do not state that the wishes of Jesus are to be violated. It was the application of the procedures that was the problem. When all of us have a situation that appears to be a moral dilemma it is best to ask ourselves that question we hear so often, "What would Jesus do?". Once we have satisfied ourselves that we have answered that question then we can act accordingly.

And when we do act accordingly, we comply with faith-based morality. But even when we do observe faith-based morality we, as flawed human beings, cannot be the judge of another person's faith or holiness, which depends on the faith-filled fervor and thoughts of another. God alone is the Judge of our faith and holiness.

Chapter 6 --- The Role Of Mission Honduras International

This chapter will be one of blame but also one of praise. Some blame is deserved by Mission Honduras International (MHI) for their handling of the APUFRAM Honduran situation, albeit they were confronted with some very difficult decisions. There will be praise for what they have done and what they are doing today in Liberia.

As I stated at the beginning of Chapter 3, the letter I received from MHI in early July, 2009, surprised me for a number of reasons. Some have already been noted. One additional reason of surprise was that it is difficult to solicit funds for charitable organizations and their letter seemed to assure that future donations would be severely curtailed. But the single biggest surprise and disappointment to me was their immediate suspension of financial support that would be necessary to help the poor children of Honduras.

One of the members of the Board of Directors of MHI sent a booklet to donors and former donors in December, 2010 which was titled, "What Would You Do In My Shoes?". I made a partial response at that time and will make a longer one in this chapter.

Before I do that, let me hasten to add they did not have the lengthy hindsight to second guess themselves as I will be doing. Nor do I know how much effort and discussions actually took place that included Father Emil. The booklet does note some of the discussions the MHI board members had with their counterparts at APUFRAM.

As noted earlier the lack of funding for the poor was my major concern. Then and today it did not seem necessary as an initial step. They could have threatened the suspension of funding or even the disassociation with APUFRAM at some future date if the child protection program was not implemented. Some of that may have been done but not enough. It would have allowed all parties, including donors, to react and to take corrective actions. It seemed then and it seems today to have been a precipitous first step. It was an action that Jesus may have railed against if committed by the Pharisees. Love of our neighbor was not enough of a priority.

It also seems that MHI was bypassing the legal system of Honduras and using the Conventual Franciscans as "the judicial system". The Franciscans did attempt to adjudicate the case. That approach was improper for a number of reasons. It was bypassing the laws of Honduras and it put the Franciscans (a religious US Order) in the position of adjudicating a case against a secular foreign organization. It also did not allow due process considerations for the allegations made against foreign individuals. Finally, it put the Franciscans in an awkward position regarding the First Amendment of the US Constitution although that was probably never a consideration by either organization, although it should have been.

It does not matter whether or not MHI lacked confidence in the Honduran justice system. They should have understood that was a risk of being involved in Honduras. It seems that MHI may not have understood that APUFRAM was a secular organization. The booklet of December, 2010 seems to imply that.

Even though the board members of MHI refuse to accept the fact that there is now an adequate child protection plan in place, their initial actions, because of the pressure put on APUFRAM, may have aided in getting that improved child protection plan put into place in early 2010. There was disagreement about whether or not the plan was exactly what was agreed to but the differences seemed to be rather minor points of i dotting and t crossing. I have come to know the ones who did implement the child protection program and have confidence that they made a sincere effort to put a good plan into place.

The MHI board also initiated a lawsuit to prevent others from using what they claimed to be their donor list. I always thought Father Emil may have had as much to do in assembling the list of donors as did anyone else. In any event, trying to resolve these type secular or moral issues by using a lawsuit is not the faith-based moral way of doing it. Donors are adults and can make up their own minds on whom to support.

There are some other lesser issues involved that were not handled well but the above are to me the most serious. Although I do not understand the reasons, there seemed to be an inordinate amount of effort to block every possible cent of funding to help the children of Honduras.

I have my suspicions as to why that was the case, but they do not deserve much further writing, because they are only an opinion and relate to the e-mail that mentioned Father Emil took $600, 000 to Honduras.

Before moving on to the Liberian mission let me again add that the Board Members of MHI did not have the time I have had to evaluate matters. On the other hand maybe they should have taken more time.

The genesis of this case was Liberia, Africa. I knew very little about this mission and that is still true for me today.

I do recall getting a request to make a contribution that would be matched by one of the MHI board members and my wife and I did make a small donation at that time.

Until the MHI board letter came to us in early July, 2009, I did not know that the staff in Liberia included any Hondurans. Having spent much of my life with an organization that had some foreign operations, I appreciate somewhat how difficult it can be to understand foreign cultures.

I don't know if the person who raped the young girl in Liberia had much training and I do not know how APUFRAM selected a missionary for assignment in Liberia. I do hope that in the future they will be very careful in such selections. In fact I hope they remain in cultures they understand. They did help cause their problem.

When the people from APUFRAM in Honduras left the Liberian mission it does seem that the ongoing management of that mission was thrown into the lap of MHI. How all that came about is somewhat unknown to me. I do know that a Franciscan priest was sent to investigate the circumstances surrounding the rape case, but it seemed that the investigation was similar to what a prosecutor's office might conduct without the input from the perspective of the defendants.

Nevertheless, the MHI board is to be commended for assuring the ongoing viability of that mission. Considering that much of their own funding had been severely reduced, one has to assume that one of the wealthy members of that Board has invested much of his personal assets in that mission.

No matter what my thoughts are regarding the actions MHI took in Honduras, the mission work being done by them in Liberia, is praiseworthy. All of us humans are flawed and all of us have the opportunities to do good in the world. The MHI Board is doing exemplary work in Liberia and no doubt at some large personal financial sacrifices.

My suspicions regarding the reasons for their excessive concern to cut off all funding to Honduras may also have had something to do with the fact that they had very little funds in their coffers after funds were taken for Honduras, That would have made the support for Liberia difficult and may have triggered some understandable annoyance. That is only an opinion on my part. If the opinion has merit, it is understandable the MHI board members would have been irritated with Father Emil and APUFRAM.

Chapter 7 --- The Conventual Franciscans Involvement

$\mathcal{M}$y elementary school years were spent in the small Missouri community of Berger. The first priest I can recall was the pastor of the Catholic Church in that small community. He was the pastor of that small parish throughout my elementary eight grades. His name was Father Roger Niemeyer, OFM. He was a Franciscan priest of the Sacred Heart Province, which is now located in St. Louis. He was an outstanding priest and role model. He influenced the lives of many students in that small parish, including myself.

Following graduation from that elementary school, I attended the minor seminary of the Franciscans located in Westmont, Illinois. The Franciscans have played a significant role in the life of my family and me. I have relatives and friends who are Franciscans. That background with the Franciscans has made this case and the writing of this chapter something less than a pleasant experience.

Of all the actions involved in this case, those of the Conventual Franciscans are most mystifying to this author. They have claimed that I do not have a significant amount of the facts in this case to draw conclusions. That is somewhat true as to certain aspects of this story, but I am not opining on areas that are unknown to me.

The lessons that their founder, St. Francis of Assisi, attempted to teach the world regarding peace, seemed to be set aside. The reason for their actions, to a large degree, have been shrouded in confidentiality, but the measures they have taken are hard to explain from a faith-based moral standpoint.

As much or more than others, the Conventual Franciscans seemed to play the role of the Pharisees in this case. I have tried at length to convince myself that there were some extreme circumstances that may have justified their positions on matters, but I can think of none. I believe that, because nothing, in my opinion, justifies countermanding the wishes of our Lord as regards our treatment of the poor.

Given that Father Emil is a member of the Conventual Franciscans, it would seem that his brother friars would have done everything possible to have been of assistance to him. But the opposite seemed to be the case. The December, 2010, MHI booklet indicated that his superiors had issues with his ministry prior to the incident in Liberia. Some of those issues also revolved around rumors of sexual abuse alleged to have been committed in the past by APUFRAM members in Honduras. Maybe that played a role in their actions, but I do not know.

Their efforts, including the suspension of funding, seemed to have been coordinated with the MHI Board and there is nothing wrong with that. What was wrong about both efforts was the failure to involve or inform secular authorities. It appears that they did not know they were dealing with a secular organization. If they did know, it makes their actions even more inexcusable.

In Chapter 3, correspondence to me by the Franciscans is duplicated. The question I asked most often of MHI and the Franciscans was, "What about this case justifies harming the poor of Honduras?". They have never answered the question. The Provincial of the Franciscans normal response was that he was following the standards of the USCCB and the procedures of his Order. Since they do not answer the question, one can only wonder if their answer, which refers to standards and procedures, means that they placed a higher priority on those standards and procedures than they placed on the teaching of our Lord or if the latter lacked sufficient consideration.

Their answer also did not and does not explain why such a major effort was made to cut off all avenues of funding to APUFRAM, which was needed to continue their operations for the poor. As noted in the prior chapter, MHI had other options to deal with the allegations and so did the Franciscans. Compassion, kindness, understanding and all the other attributes St. Paul notes of the spirit appear to have been set aside.

In fairness to the Franciscans, they live their daily lives under a different set of rules than do most of us. They also subject themselves to a different form of governance than the rest of us. Their lives to a large degree are carried out in a far more autocratic environment, than are most citizens of this nation. In their correspondence to me and others they frequently referred to those rules and to other procedures that governed their actions. Their form of governance serves them very well in most circumstances.

However, in this case, in my opinion, an excessive obedience to their rules was a major reason for their actions that ended up harming the poor. Does that justify harming the poor? No, but it may help explain their actions. That unfortunately was the problem Jesus had with the Pharisees. They too had an excessive observance to their rules. Mercy and compassion were too often forgotten.

The Franciscans in this case decided to act as prosecutor, judge and jury. Given their autocratic environment, that too is understandable. However, that does not conform their process with that of our nation's justice system. In this case it also did not conform to the wishes of our Lord.

After the many years that APUFRAM was in existence, the Franciscans should have known that it was structured as a secular organization under the laws of Honduras. The Franciscans' intrusion into the affairs of APUFRAM is difficult to explain. It was legally questionable for them to believe they could bring about justice better than the civil justice system. At a minimum, they should have involved Honduran authorities in the early stages of this case.

As this chapter is being written it has been more than two years since the Franciscans claimed they had credible allegations of sexual abuse within the APUFRAM organization, but there still has been no investigation. They also have refused to disclose those allegations or turn them over to another risk management organization to investigate. To most observers, those two decisions would seem to say that the allegations were not given adequate priority. At the time this is being written, it is likely that APUFRAM may never permit an investigation by the Franciscans which they at one point had welcomed. A great deal of friction exists between the two.

It may be just as well for the Franciscans, that they did not perform an investigation. It would have been an investigation against secular individuals, who belong to a secular foreign organization. Even if one assumes that they had personnel who were capable of performing a criminal investigation, what would they have done with the results of such an investigation? They have no standing to investigate such a case and no standing to prosecute such a case. One can only assume they did not understand the ramifications of the investigation they were going to undertake. It appears that they were beyond their area of authority.

As noted earlier, the Franciscans also demanded that Father Emil submit himself to an Order of Obedience whereby he would also divorce himself from APUFRAM. I have been informed that based upon the recommendation of a canon lawyer, Father Emil refused to comply with the order. Although I do know Father Emil and do communicate with him on occasion, I am not certain of his motives and therefore it would be unfair for me to comment at great length. Within the governance rules of the Franciscans much of those issues are carried out confidentially. I have no doubt that the Franciscans have every right to expect obedience from one of their friars if the order meets faith-based moral standards.

I don't know if the question of the Obedience Order failing to comply with faith-based moral standards entered into Father Emil's decision. It may be that he believes he must answer and observe the wishes of a higher authority. He has stated that his Order forced him to choose between two of his lifelong goals. One goal was to be a Franciscan priest and the other to help the poor of Latin America. He goes on to state that he has chosen to remain with the poor. That undoubtedly has been a painful decision for him. His decision to remain with the poor has made things more complicated for his Order and has added complexity to the entire case.

After my numerous requests to explain why this case justified harming the poor, the Provincial of the Franciscans has stopped corresponding with me. Toward the end of his communications with me he did say that the case with Father Emil had to be resolved before more would be done by them regarding the investigation of APUFRAM. Why that is necessary, he did not explain. That position continues to harm the poor.

In his December, 2009, correspondence, the Provincial made references to "putting the entire ministry at risk", when referring to additional concerns about APUFRAM. He did not mention that the "ministry" (which is in fact a secular organization) involved 1000 poor children having the opportunity for a better life. Initially he told me they had enough reserves to survive for a period of time but those references soon ended.

It is a fair and proper moral question to keep asking why this case justified harming the poor as well as asking what Jesus would have done. The Franciscans should have asked themselves those questions before taking the actions they took. On a number of occasions they have insisted that they took the proper steps in this matter.

If the allegations were of such magnitude that they warranted an instant investigation it would seem that such an investigation for the protection of the children at risk would have been undertaken as soon as possible. But there has neither been an investigation performed for the protection of the children nor has there been any revocation of the funding restrictions. As noted earlier, one is only left to wonder how high the welfare of poor children was and is on the priority list of the Franciscans. Just because they have a separate issue with Father Emil, does not justify the continued restriction on funding for APUFRAM.

During this case, as I have also noted earlier, there were many pleas by me to all parties to communicate with one another and to follow the example of St. Francis to try to help bring about peace. My efforts in that regard continue, but to date have been of no avail. I blame all parties for a lack of such efforts, but it did seem that efforts toward peace were attempted in the fall of 2009 and that the Franciscans as much as anyone else took actions to preclude peace.

They seem to have forgotten the beautiful words of the wonderful Saint from Assisi:

Lord make me an instrument of you peace;
Where there is hatred let me sow love;
Where there is injury, pardon;
Where there is doubt, faith;
Where there is despair, hope;
Where there is darkness, light;
and where there is sadness, joy.
Grant that I may not so much seek to be consoled as to
console;
To be understood as to understand;
To be loved as to love;
For it is in giving that we receive,
It is in pardoning that we are pardoned,
and it is in dying that we are born to eternal life.

In my view, it should matter that Father Emil via APUFRAM has dedicated most of his entire adult life to the poor in Honduras, helped 30,000 children escape a life of deprivation, helped provide funds to build or refurbish as many as 15 churches a year, provides financial assistance to priests who are poor or work in poor areas, provides pastoral workers for those in rural years and spent weekend after weekend saying several Masses for many in rural areas of Honduras. And it was through APUFRAM that he hoped to continue his vision for the poor once he left this earth.

I hope and pray daily that the Franciscans can understand what Father Emil has accomplished in his work for the Lord and that they will heed the word of our Lord to help the poor. The past forty years of working among the very poor do not seem to cast Father Emil as a Pharisee. As with all of us it is our Savior who will pass final judgment on Padre Emilio.

The religious hierarchy of the Catholic Church has been in a very difficult period trying to deal with the clerical sexual abuse issue, and I do have sympathy for the Franciscans in this case. It seems that the hierarchy is criticized no matter what they do. Even though such cases are very difficult, they do not justify a departure from the faith-based morality given to us by our Lord.

Chapter 8 --- The United States Conference Of Catholic Bishops

The United States Conference of Catholic Bishops (USCCB) is headquartered in Washington D.C. at 3211 Fourth St. N.E. It has some of the characteristics of other institutions located in our nation's capital. It is somewhat bureaucratic, somewhat insular and somewhat provincial. But, thus far, moats do not surround the building and drawbridges are not deemed necessary. Within this building many of the standards, procedures and rules which govern some of the secular aspects of the Catholic Church in the United States are drafted and subsequently promulgated. In between those activities the Bishops of the Church occasionally gather and vote aye or nay on these standards, procedures and rules.

There may be a little hyperbole in the above paragraph but not much and maybe none at all.

In a discussion with a director of the office of one of our fine Bishops, he concurred with some of what was just noted. It is not intended as a harsh criticism. That is the way it is with big organizations. In my working days, I was the number three person in a multi-billion dollar organization and that experience makes me all too familiar with the bureaucratic problem. My guess is that many in that organization leveled the same criticism of bureaucracy against yours truly.

In that type atmosphere it is all too easy to take on some aspects of the Pharisees. *Hey, we have some pretty tough charters, standards, procedures, rules, and regulations around here. You say we caused hundreds of children to be harmed in Honduras. Maybe the group down the hall can help you, unless, of course they have rules against that.* Breaking through the barriers of such an organization is very difficult, given the procedures that govern them. Getting them to change something harmful in a Memorandum almost surely requires the help of the Holy Spirit. I continue to seek his help in this case.

In Chapter 3, there is the duplication of the memo sent to all the Bishops in the United States in regard to the funding restriction placed on Father Emil and APUFRAM. I have tried to discover the process that the memo went through within the USCCB's offices and even that is difficult.

When he was still communicating with me, the Provincial of the Franciscans, who asked that the memo be circulated, told me he sent it to the USCCB Secretariat of the Child and Youth Protection. The very cooperative Executive Director of that Office advised me that she did not receive it. This particular Executive Director recently left the USCCB. She was the most helpful of any person within the USCCB. But as she told me, her hands were tied relative to getting the memo revoked. *Yes, we do have rules. Maybe the office down the hall can help you.*

The person who signed the memo on behalf of the USCCB was a Msgr. Ronny Jenkins. At that time he was an Associate General Secretary. He is now the General Secretary. In a more secular organization that title would be Executive Director.

He is no doubt a very busy individual. He has been the recipient of numerous e-mails and letters written by me and copied on many more. His number of responses. Zero. A Pharisee? I doubt that he is. But, he is governed by many rules and procedures, and in this case may be a victim of the bureaucracy he oversees. It may be that he now understands the problems with the memo but knows that that he cannot overturn that memo, no matter if it is morally flawed. Religious Orders are to a large degree independent from the USCCB even though they circulated the memo on behalf of the Franciscans.

A source at the USCCB has informed me that the USCCB was not required to issue the memo if it did not think it was proper. Without any input from the

Monsignor I can't be sure, but he may have merely handled the memo as a very routine matter. He may have done no evaluation of it and just went ahead and circulated it. It would seem that someone in the USCCB would review such memos for moral and legal correctness. If that was done in this case I do not know.

There have been numerous clerical sexual abuse cases and he may not have seen anything unusual about it. I am giving him the benefit of the doubt since it should not have taken much review time to know that APUFRAM was a secular and foreign organization. That alone should have alerted him or someone below him who may have reviewed the memo.

The memo of 12/22/09 now seems to be the captive of a Catch 22 situation. The USCCB staff indicates they can do nothing to revoke the memo without receiving such authority from the Franciscans and the Franciscans state they will do nothing until the issues with Father Emil are resolved. So even though the USCCB standards on Child Protection have now been implemented by APUFRAM for almost two years, the restrictions on funding continue and poor children unnecessarily are forced to suffer. That is not my view of what Jesus would have done.

One of the sad parts of this sad story is that we still don't know and may never know if anyone in Honduras did anything wrong, but the procedures, rules, etc. etc. continue to allow the restriction on funding to remain in place.

Now to the Bishops. I have probably contacted somewhere between 30 and 50 Bishops about this case. Initially, it was the Bishops of those dioceses where Father Emil visited to raise funds. I have heard from none of them and did not really expect that. I merely wanted to inform them of the circumstances of the case. I have kept my own Bishop informed and he has not responded although I have also not written to him in that vein. I am somewhat disappointed that he has decided to remain on the sideline.

There have been three Archbishops who have responded, one of whom is a Cardinal. All have responded to one of my letters. Two have volunteered that they would or would have someone look into the case. The third Archbishop went further. He not only responded, but through a mutual friend, I was able to visit with him for a few minutes. He urged me to continue my pursuit of getting the USCCB memo revoked. All three that did respond have positions as heads of major archdioceses and no doubt have huge time consuming positions in the Church. Their responsiveness will always be appreciated and remembered.

They may also have run into the bureaucracy of their own organization and in all likelihood, they have little if any jurisdiction in this case because it involves an "independent" religious Order. There are those rules and procedures again. It is too bad that the rules permitted the memo to be circulated. What could be done in the way of circulating the memo, cannot now easily be undone without the consent of the Provincial of the Conventual Franciscans.

Given that the Provincial has stated that the case with Father Emil must first be resolved, the memo may be outstanding for a very long time and under the circumstances, its revocation may never happen. Hopefully, that will not be the case. The poor children of Honduras deserve a higher level of consideration.

I cannot read the minds of the rest of the Bishops that have been contacted about this case. Some may have asked the USCCB staff for clarification of the case. but I simply don't know. They probably just ignored my letters, since it was not their problem. What I do know is that the memo is still outstanding after more than two years and as long as that is the case, justice as determined by faith-based morality appears not to be served.

It would be wrong for me to classify the Bishops as being apathetic in regards to the case. However, the word passive would be appropriate. When enough of our Bishops are informed of the moral flaws of this case, and that it is being harmful to poor children, they are in the position to provide spiritual leadership and make attempts to get wrongs corrected. Letting this memo linger on is not a demonstration of moral leadership. It is only my opinion, but if the Bishops felt strongly about this case they could probably exert enough pressure to have it revoked.

It is quite likely that the memo was circulated without question and both the USCCB staff and the Bishops now find themselves in a position of not being able to easily undo what was done. In my corporate days, that would have generated a question about procedures, especially considering, that it is approaching two years since APUFRAM implemented the USCCB standards for child protection.

My questions to each of the Bishops are the same as those which I have posed to the Provincial of the Franciscans. What is it about this case that justifies harming the poor? I would also ask them what they think Jesus would do if He were made aware of this case.

Our Lord occasionally expects us to be pro-active. When we do nothing we accept things that are wrong. The good Samaritan chose a different path. In this case a young couple decided to become good Samaritans. Their efforts are covered in Chapter 10.

Another group, APUFRAM International, was also formed to aid the children of Honduras. Their struggles and concerns are covered in the next chapter.

Chapter 9 --- *Apufram International*

$\mathcal{D}$uring the period that the MHI Board was considering suspension of funding and shortly thereafter a small group of people decided that it was not right to suspend the funding for the poor children of Honduras. They began establishing an organization which would be a vehicle to solicit and remit funds on behalf of APUFRAM.

My recollection is that it was Joan Pharr, the former MHI Board member, who advised me that this group was forming. She introduced me to Mary Eckart, who was one of the people trying to form APUFRAM International and who, along with the help of others, incorporated the non-profit organization in Arkansas about the time that the funding for APUFRAM was suspended by MHI. Sometime later I became familiar with Tom Crea who served as the organization's first Executive Director. Their only purpose was to do fundraising for the poor children of Honduras.

They would run into many obstacles in their endeavors. The major one was the USCCB memo which included them. They were told they could not use Father Emil's name in fundraising. They were also sued by MHI regarding the use of the donor's list. But they continued to persist in their efforts. It has always seemed strange to me that they were targeted as a group in the USCCB memo. None of the members had done anything wrong and the results of prohibiting them from fundraising was to harm the children of Honduras. They were not linked to any sexual wrongdoing in Honduras. Restricting their fundraising efforts, was not a merciful way of improving the safe environment for the poor children of Honduras.

They have endured the obstacles and continue to operate. They have managed to continue collecting enough funds to support about 250 to 300 of the 700 to 800 children that APUFRAM can presently afford to help on an annual basis. Father Emil continues fundraising efforts which now flow through APUFRAM International.

In the past year I have had the opportunity to meet Joan Pharr, who is not directly involved with APUFRAM International, although a supporter, and Mary Eckart, who is the Treasurer. I am impressed with their dedication to the efforts they make to help the poor.

I have also become familiar with the names of those who serve on the APUFRAM International Board of Directors. All of them have been to Honduras and all are dedicated to helping Father Emil and the poor children of Honduras. If those who choose to block their efforts are pharisaical in this case then the people of APUFRAM International are the disciples for the poor. They have chosen not to be deterred by those who believe that rigid and excessive application of standards regarding clerical sexual abuse through methods that harm the poor makes moral sense.

In June, 2011 the Board of Directors of APUFRAM International passed a resolution enumerating the reasons the USCCB memo is morally flawed and unjust. That resolution was made available to me and states the following:

"APUFRAM INTERNATIONAL

BOARD RESOLUTION DATED JUNE 23, 2011

At a meeting held June 23, 2011 the Board of Directors of APUFRAM International presented and adopted the following resolution in regards to the United States Conference of Catholic Bishops (USCCB) Memorandum (MEMO) dated December 22, 2009, being a non-endorsement of any fundraising in the United States by Father Emil Cook, APUFRAM and APUFRAM International, a copy of which is attached hereto: (note - it is included in Chapter 3)

WHEREAS: The MEMO violates the wishes of our Lord to help the poor which should be the prime moral consideration,

WHEREAS: The MEMO has caused APUFRAM to reduce its support for the very poor young people it serves, resulting, since the distribution of the MEMO, in between 250 and 300 children annually not being given the opportunity of an education with hope for the future,

WHEREAS: The MEMO has precluded APUFRAM from constructing or refurbishing 10 to 15 churches per year as it did previously, at the direct request of individual priests and bishops in Honduras,

WHEREAS: The MEMO has forced APUFRAM to drastically reduce its support of pastoral workers, who provide catechetical instructions to remote rural areas of Honduras,

WHEREAS: APUFRAM is a foreign secular organization and APUFRAM International is a secular US organization and therefore not subjected to the rules and procedures of either the Conventual Franciscans of Our Lady of Consolation or the USCCB and which has been acknowledged by the USCCB in a letter dated January 12, 2010,

WHEREAS: The action by the Conventual Franciscans and the USCCB has legal considerations inasmuch as it harmed secular organizations,

WHEREAS: There have been no allegations of any clerical sexual abuse and thus the lack of such allegations should not have subjected APUFRAM to either the USCCB or Conventual Franciscans' standards and rules regarding such abuses,

WHEREAS: Any allegations of any sexual abuse against APUFRAM or APUFRAM personnel are allegations of a crime in the secular world and should, by dictate of the Vatican issued in April 2010, be referred to Honduran civil authorities,

WHEREAS: Civil authorities in Honduras have not been made aware of any allegations against APUFRAM or APUFRAM personnel,

WHEREAS: The Conventual Franciscans have inappropriately acted as prosecutor, judge and jury against secular organizations and in a manner that violates the United States justice system regarding separation of church and state and due process,

WHEREAS: APUFRAM has operated continuously since 1990 under a comprehensive child protection program required by the country of Honduras, earning positive reviews after annual mandated inspections at each of its sites by the Honduran Institute of Children and the Family (IHNFA) and receiving the prestigious National Prize of Human Rights in 2008,

WHEREAS: The Conventual Franciscans acted precipitously in requesting on December 20, 2009 (just at the Christmas and end of year giving season)

that the USCCB act to issue its MEMO inasmuch as APUFRAM had already drafted on request of the Franciscans and was about to present a newly rewritten Child Protection Plan which met the USCCB standards,

WHEREAS: The MEMO states that the basis for the MEMO was that APUFRAM had not demonstrated to the Conventual Franciscans that adequate safe environment programs had been enforced at its locations, albeit the Conventual Franciscans well knew that APUFRAM was in the process of redrafting its Child Protection Plan after a meeting in November 2009 with the Franciscans in El Salvador at which APUFRAM presented a first draft of its revised plan,

WHEREAS: In January, 2010 APUFRAM presented an approved whistleblower policy to the Conventual Franciscans and in February 2010 presented the final version of its Child Protection Plan to the Conventual Franciscans, a fact the Conventual Franciscans have never acknowledged,

WHEREAS: APUFRAM implemented the Child Protection Plan in early 2010 with the participation of an independent review board made up of a priest who heads Caritas in Honduras, a Jesuit priest, and two prominent business leaders, with an independent organization to monitor the program including periodic examination of locked complaint boxes and conduct of impromptu interviews of personnel and students, and also with implementation of a child protection training program for both staff and beneficiaries at all its sites,

WHEREAS: The Conventual Franciscans claim to hold credible reports of abuse within APUFRAM but have never begun the investigation of APUFRAM as promised in late 2009, the results of which APUFRAM agreed to accept, and also refused to provide the allegations to an independent third party risk management company (Praesidium, Inc.) so that they could conduct an independent investigation,

WHEREAS: By their refusal to conduct an investigation or to cooperate with a respected third party willing to conduct an investigation, the Conventual Franciscans have thereby allowed unsubstantiated allegations to be widely disseminated without providing APUFRAM the opportunity to prove that these allegations are false,

WHEREAS: APUFRAM's position has always been that they will accept and cooperate with investigations based on the national laws of Honduras and carried out by competent authorities of Honduras at any time and when there may be a formal complaint,

WHEREAS; The Conventual Franciscans have recently stated in a letter to an APUFRAM International board member that the reason for not following through with the promised investigation of child abuse allegations within APUFRAM was the lack of an agreed upon child protection policy,

WHEREAS; In conclusion, the MEMO was requested by the Conventual Franciscans on the stated basis that APUFRAM had not demonstrated that adequate safe environment programs had been enforced at its locations, and since the Conventual Franciscans knew that APUFRAM's existing Child Protection Plan was then being drafted to make it consistent with USCCB guidelines, and since only weeks after the MEMO was issued, APUFRAM presented a final draft of its plan to the Conventual Franciscans without response, and since there has been no investigation of alleged child abuse cases within APUFRAM and no such cases have been referred to civil investigative authorities, a conclusion can be drawn that the Conventual Franciscans have intentionally chosen to allow fundraising restrictions that the MEMO imposes to issue and to persist without factual or moral justification.

THEREFORE BE IT

RESOLVED: That the Board of Directors of APUFRAM International hereby requests both the USCCB and the Conventual Franciscans to immediately withdraw the MEMO."

Some of the above was reviewed in Chapter 7, but some details were not known to me until I saw the resolution. Although, the final supposition is just that, it sets forth very well the reasons the USCCB MEMO should be revoked.

As long as the MEMO is outstanding, it will make it more difficult to raise funds for APUFRAM. When Father Emil does his fundraising in the United States it is primarily done through Catholic churches and Catholic organizations. Because of the MEMO some of those as well as many individuals are reluctant to be financially supportive or to even let Father Emil do fundraising.

The lawsuit which was settled with MHI also makes it more difficult for APUFRAM International to work with former donors. The settlement requires certain conditions be met before former donors can be contacted.

It spite of the hurdles that are in their way, APUFRAM International as noted earlier makes it possible for about 250 children annually to obtain an education.

Chapter 10 --- Special Missions Foundation

Because of the actions of two people at Special Missions Foundation, this chapter is a pleasure to write. Special Missions Foundation is primarily the work of a husband and wife; Jerry Thompson and Sandra Romero de Thompson, Ph.D. Sandra is a native of Honduras.

The purpose of Special Missions Foundation, which is located in Texas, is to connect financial and human resources with specific humanitarian and development needs in Honduras. They also serve as facilitators for those who wish to financially support projects in the country and need an umbrella legal structure and an accountable and transparent process.

They also sponsor an annual conference in the town of Copan Ruinas, Honduras. Its aim is to present and exchange information on current and proposed grassroots volunteer projects to help the people of Honduras.

My first knowledge of Special Missions Foundation was about a month after we received the letter from MHI advising us that they were suspending funding to APUFRAM. At that time APUFRAM International was not a tax-exempt organization for donors. Special Missions Foundation volunteered to accept contributions from donors which provided tax deductibility.

After a confusing letter from MHI, which cast doubt on Special Missions Foundation willingness to accept donations on behalf of APUFRAM, I decided to speak to Jerry Thompson. He assured me that they were accepting such donations.

At this point I should add that the Thompsons are not Catholics and I believe the only non-Catholics of the twenty or more people I have come to know who were involved in this case. They are extraordinarily faithful Christians. They accomplished more for the protection of children who would go through the APUFRAM program than all the people combined who believed it was necessary to suspend funding for the poor to accomplish the same thing.

Jerry attended the meetings between the parties during which attempts at accords were made, and thereby learned what MHI and the Conventual Franciscans wanted in the way of child protection. When those efforts failed, the Conventual Franciscans requested the

USCCB to issue the non-endorsement of fund raising memo in December, 2009.

Without any fanfare, the Thompsons proceeded to work with APUFRAM and by March of 2010 they had implemented the Child Protection Plan in accord with USCCB standards. That has not been acknowledged by others, but given the history of this case, I trust and accept the Thompson's representation that it did. Sandra was also to become involved in the follow-up reviews to ensure that APUFRAM was in accord with the Child Protection program.

Faith is a special gift from our Lord. Faith does not require that we belong to any specific religion. It also does not require that one belong to any specific religion to act in accord with faith-based morality. The Thompsons in my view have demonstrated great faith throughout their involvement in this case. They had a single-minded goal, which I am sure was pleasing to our Lord. They just wanted to help the poor children of Honduras. It was a simple and faithful goal.

They would go beyond just implementing the Child Protection Plan. The Thompsons understood the importance of attempting to clear the good name of APUFRAM and of uncovering, and resolving, any possible wrongdoings. They also understood that an investigation by the Conventual Franciscans might not happen in a timely manner, if ever. They contacted Praesidium, Inc, a risk management firm, that had conducted many investigations. They have done investigations for a large number of Catholic organizations, including the Franciscans.

In order to conduct the investigation, it would be necessary to have the allegations that were possessed by only MHI and the Conventual Franciscans. Both, for inexplicable reasons, refused to provide the allegations to the risk management firm. It is inexplicable because the safety of the children was the very reason for the USCCB memo. Here was the opportunity to get an independent investigation done by a well know firm, and the opportunity to again seek out or clear any of the wrongdoers, but the opportunity was squandered.

The Thompsons would also convince APUFRAM to hire a very reputable firm to train the employees of APUFRAM in order to make the employees aware and conscious of the importance of good child protection and safety.

If the approach taken by the Thompsons had been taken by MHI and the Conventual Franciscans this book would never have been written. The case could have ended quickly. If those two parties had worked harder at bringing about a safer environment for children in Honduras, by using kind and peaceful techniques as did the Thompsons, much acrimony would have been avoided. They too could have accomplished what the Thompsons did accomplish.

The Thompsons did what some priests, Bishops and members of the USCCB refused to do. They became good Samaritans for the poor children of Honduras. They continue to work toward that simple goal of making life better for those children who desperately need help. Fortunately, the Thompsons would not allow themselves to be hindered with the many rules and laws of the Pharisees. They understand the Lord's wishes for mercy and compassion.

When it was virtually impossible to get any tax-exempt funding to APUFRAM through any other method, the Thompsons made their Foundation available. When no one else would implement the Children Protection Plan, the Thompsons did just that. When no one else tried to ascertain if any wrongdoing took place in Honduras by APUFRAM members, the Thompsons attempted to get a risk management firm to conduct an investigation. The Thompsons also suggested and APUFRAM hired a firm to implement training that would help ensure a safe environment.

The Thompsons will have my never ending admiration. They deserve the label of good Samaritans.

Chapter 11 ~~~ The Results Of Secular~Based Morality

The sequence of events that led to the circulation of the USCCB memo seemed to me, to be one flawed moral judgment and decision after another. It began with APUFRAM sending someone to Liberia who should not have been there. I don't know how much review APUFRAM did in selecting the person who was sent to Liberia. It is difficult for someone of one culture to adapt to another culture. Not everyone, is capable of making that type transition.

After the rape of the young Liberian girl, there were a series of efforts made to circumvent Liberian law. It may be true that there is a certain amount of corruption in Liberia, but those are risks that one assumes when they establish a mission. Father Emil and APUFRAM seem to have tried to resolve the sexual abuse case in their own manner while MHI and the Conventual Franciscans tried a different tact. I do not know which side took the moral high ground in their search for justice. But why the Franciscans decided to insert themselves into the affairs of foreign countries and foreign organizations is hard to understand.

Why MHI knew so little about APUFRAM before this case is also hard to understand since it was their only benefactor to my knowledge. Why they then became excessively involved is more understandable. After knowing too little about APUFRAM, they claimed to uncover additional cases of sexual abuse relating to the mission in Honduras that may or may not ever be verified. I don't know why the proper authorities have not been informed, although one member of the MHI Board informed me that they did not trust the Honduras justice system. That is understandable, but I do not think the Franciscans were the proper ones to attempt to pursue justice, especially since APUFRAM is a secular organization.

The Franciscans have said that the allegations against members of APUFRAM were credible but I do not know what that means. It is both morally and legally wrong to let those allegations languish. It is simply not proper to make allegations and then ignore them for years. These allegations have harmed the reputation of APUFRAM and members within the APUFRAM organization. If there are charges of a criminal nature they should be turned over to the proper authorities.

Even though APUFRAM and APUFRAM International have some ties to the Catholic Church they are nonetheless secular organizations. It made no moral or legal sense for the Franciscans to come to the decision that they could perform as prosecutor, judge and jury for the allegations against APUFRAM that surfaced after the Liberian incident. APUFRAM is not only a secular organization but a foreign organization. Within the governance of Catholic church organizations it may be appropriate to apply justice in an autocratic manner. In secular situations it is not appropriate.

This was not a case of applying faith-based morality to a situation. Just because some secular type rules are in place within the Catholic church for handling clerical sexual abuse case does not make those rules matters of faith and morals. In this case they were applied in a secular manner. The actions taken have nothing to do with the faith and moral teachings of Scripture or Apostolic Tradition. One secular mistake seemed to follow another

During the past two years it has puzzled me greatly as to what caused both the Board of Mission Honduras International and the Conventual Franciscans to take the harshest steps possible to deal with Father Emil and APUFRAM. Yes, they may have been hoping to make changes within APUFRAM, but the withholding of funds as a first step seemed likely from the beginning to lead to the mess that has ensued. Was there something that merited such a reaction? I say no because our Lord wants us to be a compassionate people and certainly did not want us to harm the poor. The love of one another He commanded was not apparent.

I once made a comment about the harshness of the approach to the Provincial of the Conventual Franciscans when we were still exchanging e-mails. As noted earlier, he referred to procedures that were to be followed in sexual abuse cases and he referred to the suspension of a priest's ministry being part of those procedures. I reviewed a number of such procedures and did find that they did indeed make reference to a suspension of ministry. That however seems more appropriate in cases where the clergyman has been charged with sexual abuse and the rationale is to prevent him from committing further sexual abuse.

That rationale did not apply in this case inasmuch as Father Emil has not been charged with any sexual abuse. It seemed a stretch to apply the procedure relating to clerical sexual abuse in a manner that prevented him from raising funds for the poor, which admittedly was a part of his ministry. It was even more of a stretch to then add APUFRAM and APUFRAM International to the fundraising restriction. It was also legally questionable, inasmuch as they are secular organizations and one is also a foreign organization.

Their decision was also legally dubious inasmuch as they seemed to be ignoring the First Amendment of the US Constitution. They also seemed to be handing out punishment before any guilt was proven. Our legal system presumes innocence until guilt is proven. They applied justice in a manner that departs from our own justice system.

The Provincial on several occasions has mentioned that the Liberian mission was left high and financially dry by APUFRAM. That of course depends on one's perspective. Having suspended the fundraising for the children of Honduras, APUFRAM did not have enough funds to take care of all the children in Honduras much less Liberia. Whether APUFRAM deserted the mission or whether they were driven from the mission seems to depend on different interpretations of what took place. Nevertheless, the actions of MHI in continuing the operations of the Liberian mission are laudable.

It may be that the motives for the harsh action will never be known. As one goes through various scenarios, the one that may make some sense is that Father Emil did take funds with him to Honduras around the time he learned that fundraising suspensions were to be put into place. That may have caused a reaction. I don't know. He has never discussed that with me so it is purely a conjecture on my part. Suffice it to say, the harsh measure of sealing off the funds flowing to Honduras seemed to be aimed at both Father Emil and

APUFRAM. The real motivation for that action may never be known.

Regardless of the why, it is difficult to assign a faith-based motive to the fundraising suspension. There simply are no obvious faith-based reasons that would permit measures to be taken that were aimed at harming the poor. There may have been sins of a sexual nature committed in Honduras and by someone in or associated with the APUFRAM organization, but we do not know. That does not justify harming the poor. We know that in Haiti there were serious sexual abuses but the US Bishops pleaded for us to financially support the poor of that nation and that was a faith-based moral thing to do.

We can only assign the restrictions on funding to secular-based moral reasoning. It does seem that some of the venom was directed at Father Emil. He has never been charged with anything more than "covering up" or "should have known" type allegations. There may be truth in those accusations but they are not founded in faith-based morality. It may also be that Father Emil was being protective of someone that to him was family. That may not have made his trying to protect the person legally proper, but I am not about to judge such actions morally. That is rightly left to our Lord to judge.

But some charges were also directed at the APUFRAM organization. Given the way they were handled those charges may never remain more than allegations. There has been no due process of those allegations. Within this country they have no doubt damaged the reputation of APUFRAM. Based on a reliable source, it now seems that APUFRAM may never accede to a US organization conducting an investigation. Given the poor treatment they have received from MHI, the Conventual Franciscans and the USCCB staff that is understandable.

When people or organizations decide to follow a secular-based moral path, it is easy to stray from the path of the teaching of Jesus. It is for our Lord to judge if any of us in this case have been guilty of that which Jesus accused the Pharisees. The rules and procedures that were applied may be fine, but the application of those rules are difficult to find in the teaching of Jesus.

Given that the two sides have at times had acrimonious exchanges and been involved in a lawsuit, it is not difficult to say that Jesus may not have approved of the actions of both. Secular-based morality too often does not have faith as a basis for action.

We can list some of the faith-based moral wrongs that have been associated with this case.

1 - The poor, especially children have been harmed, because the restriction on funding has reduced the number of children by about 250 per year who

could otherwise have been part of the APUFRAM program.

2 - The reputations of APUFRAM and people within the APUFRAM organization have been damaged through allegations that have been permitted to exist for a long period of time. They should be pursued or dropped.

3 - Love of neighbor has not been demonstrated.

4- Mercy and compassion have been lacking.

5 - The reputation of a priest has been damaged by innuendo and by charges that are not clear, although confidentiality may be a large part of the reason. If sexual abuse charges are involved they should be turned over to the proper authorities. Nevertheless, he is subject to the rules of his Order.

6- Reduction in funding has made it impossible to build churches in Honduras and thereby has harmed the ability to bring faith in our Lord to more people. Before the restriction on funding APUFRAM was able to build or refurbish from 10 to 15 churches each year.

7 - Reduction in funding has made it impossible to provide as much catechetical instructions to children and others in the rural areas of Honduras.

When we apply procedures, rules, standards or laws in a way that do not find such applications in the teaching of Jesus we fail to observe faith-based morality. Was that not the problem Jesus had with the Pharisees? He said, "Observe their laws but not their example".

Chapter 12 --- A Better Path Via Faith-Based Morality

This is a sad story. It is especially sad, because so many people who should have understood the best path to follow at various decision points decided against following that path. The path of faith-based morality was an option many times and yet it was ignored many times. The answer as to why that was the case is difficult to understand.

When we humans are able to identify faith-based morality, we can be assured that following such a course of action is the right course of action. When we follow the path Jesus has shown us, we know that it is the right path. It is the faith-based moral path. Sometimes, our sinful human intelligence rejects the spiritual wisdom of our soul. Life is a perpetual struggle for each of us to return to that faith-based moral path.

As noted, there were opportunities to follow faith-based morality in this case. That opportunity always exists. It may appear that such a path would have conflicted with the procedures of the Church, but I do not believe that to be the case. If there was a conflict it would be the Church procedures that would be the problem. There are no faith-based moral errors in the wishes of our Lord to help the poor.

Sin exists in this world. It not only exists for a few but it exists for all. The rape of a young girl is a terrible sin and one that is repulsive to all of us. It is also a crime against the laws of most countries. In this case it was committed in Liberia. Because the application of justice may be suspect in Liberia, that does not automatically give individuals or an organization or a religious order the right to circumvent their justice system.

Father Emil and APUFRAM were assumed to be errant in their judgments made in the Liberian case. What little I do know about their role in that case may simply indicate that their greatest guilt was excessive compassion and mercy. In our secular parlance, it may be that they were guilty of "covering up". I am not certain that is guilt in the eyes of God. He reminded the Pharisees on several occasions to try to understand the meaning of mercy.

The Lord did not dictate the type of punishments that were to be handed out for crimes on earth. Those were the things that he would leave to Caesar. Punishment for crimes on earth are secular decisions. Our Lord was more concerned about mercy and forgiveness and less about punishment on earth. He was far more concerned with the punishment we might confront after leaving this earth.

Everything God taught us about mercy and compassion could and should have been followed in this case. He is the final judge. We simply cannot interject ourselves as purveyors of justice in international situations where we don't like the approach or the outcome of some country's justice system. We have a process for doing that. In this case, too many people decided to be the justice system. Some things need to be left to Him who provides Final Judgment.

Let us try to follow the sequence of events and see how Jesus might have wished that they be handled. Jesus was compassionate with sinners. When the crowd was about to stone a woman who had sinned he warned, "Let those without sin cast the first stone". I don't know enough of the facts of the Liberian case to decide if one side or the other had the better faith-based moral solution. Too many were trying to justify their own sense of secular-based justice on the assumption that Liberian law would not serve such justice. Casting stones was the order of the day.

Next came the allegations against APUFRAM personnel. We do not know if these actually happened. We may never know. I don't know if Jesus would have approved of the way the accusations were made and then handled. Here too, people were trying to justify their own view of secular-based justice. In this set of allegations, people again decided that the Honduran justice system could not satisfy justice so they turned to a religious order to follow a set of procedures that did not really apply to the situation. Casting stones was the order of the day.

Then came the suspension of funding; first by the MHI Board and then by the Conventual Franciscans. Of all the steps taken, this seems to have most violated the faith-based morality of our Lord. That violation of faith-based morality has been referenced numerous times in this book. We are morally wrong from a faith perspective when we do not abide by his wishes. Nothing could be much farther from his wishes than to take actions which directly harmed poor children.

The next step which seemed to violate faith-based morality was the circulation of the MEMO to Bishops by the USCCB staff which further extended the endorsement of no fundraising. Even though it was requested by the Conventual Franciscans, the USCCB staff should have exercised some precautions that would preclude the violation of the wishes of our Lord when they circulate such a MEMO.

Another violation of faith-based morality is the manner in which the parties have treated each other. The second commandment of our Lord to love our neighbor as our self seemed to be cast aside. I have always assumed that anyone who is prepared for Heaven can have no outstanding grudges against anyone when he/she passes through the pearly gates. That is not what Heaven is about. Love of Creator and love of each other will be the norm. All of us sinners will learn that moral lesson in this life or the next.

One more of the sad things about this sad story is that everyone seems to be claiming that their approach was the proper approach. It seems that someone might have at least thought the likelihood of being on the wrong side of faith-based morality existed. I used to think it was only politicians who could never admit to being wrong, but I suppose that human affliction extends to many of us. It does make one wonder about the meaning of "examination of conscience". If two sides are opposed on a moral issue, surely someone must know they are on the wrong side of the faith-based moral issue. Self-righteousness prevails.

Another sad part of the story is the passiveness with which this story has been treated by the hierarchy of my beloved Catholic Church. As noted in Chapter 8 many Bishops have been informed of this case and have also been told of the harm being done to the poor. Most, but not all, seem to view it as someone else's problems. Good Samaritans among our Bishops have been hard to find. I hasten to add that a few have indicated their concern with the case, but most of them refer the matter back to the USCCB staff where the problem originated within the USCCB.

The Bishops are in a position to correct the faults of the USCCB staff if they feel strongly about an issue. The bureaucrats within the USCCB staff should not have veto power over the Bishops and the Bishops need to provide moral leadership when the wishes of our Lord are violated within their own organization. Because of the many clerical sexual abuse cases, I have sympathy for the Bishops in this area. Nevertheless, being passive in this case is harmful.

For the want of faith-based morality many poor children have suffered needlessly. This case indicates how the very best among us can get lost in the web of secular-based morality. It is easy to go down that wrong path. It sometimes takes courage to follow the wishes of our Lord. At every step along the way of this case, that "someone", who could have been another good Samaritan, made the decision that it was not their responsibility. That may be as sad as any other part of this story.

Several of my previous books have warned how many of the ills of our society today are found in secular-based morality which too often borders on secular humanism. There is a lack of faith-based morality in regards to the sanctity of life. There is a lack of faith-based morality with respect to the sanctity of the nuclear family. The lack of faith-based morality permeates far too many actions of this nation.

It is a very sad conclusion that secular-based morality has been permitted to override faith-based morality, even by those, who have been trained to proclaim the morality of faith. They are the ones who can bring this case back on a faith-based moral path. Thus far, they have chosen a different path.

At the beginning of this book, it was noted that a goal of telling this story was to help readers be able to make decisions in the future to avoid some of the moral mistakes made in this case. That does not exclude the hierarchy of our Church.

It was also noted that life is a spiritual warfare. Life on earth is a perpetual struggle of good against evil. That is not only a cultural struggle, but also a struggle of each human being.

When we take measures, which harm the poor, we trod in an area which Jesus warned us about many times. In the Book of Exodus, the Lord warned those who oppressed widows and orphans (the poor) that such sins were "sins that cry out to heaven". Does the sin that harms the poor children of Honduras constitute a sin that cries out to heaven? I don't know, but we do know our Lord warned us about harming the poor. Sins that cry out to Heaven are frequently the collective sins of many as was true of slavery. If this case rises to a sin that cries out to Heaven, the USCCB memo does nothing to mitigate such a sin.

Sin causes spiritual pain. Much about this case caused such pain. People who were trying to do good deeds were prevented from doing them. As I became aware of, and then involved with, some of the facts of this story, it seemed that too many actions were wrong from a faith-based moral perspective and that was true. The sad part was that the wrongs being committed were by those trying to do good as best as they could define good. At times that included me.

Did the Pharisees understand that their strict and obsessive adherence to their rules caused them to violate the wishes of our Lord? I don't know the answer to that and I don't know if those of us on earth today understand adequately when we violate his wishes. I know each of us still needs to work harder to understand and observe his wishes and his commands. We need to embrace the actions of the good Samaritan and cast aside the actions of the Pharisees.

Sin is a part of God's plan for human beings. It is true that sin causes pain. But through our sins God demonstrates his love, his pity and his compassion for us sinners. Through Sacred Scripture God made known the sins of David in the Old Testament and in the New Testament we read of the sins of Mary Magdalene, St.

Peter and St. Paul. We also learn of their contrition and their subsequent great and growing love of our Lord.

We must learn to accept our own sins and the sins of others. It is through sin that we can experience what Julian of Norwich learned during one of the revelations of our Lord to her.

By contrition we are made clean, by compassion we are made ready, and by true longing we are made worthy. These are three means, as I understand, through which all souls come to heaven, those, that is to say, who have been sinners on earth and will be saved. For every sinful soul must be healed by these medicines.

Much about this case still causes pain. Much about this case still needs pharisaical actions to be exchanged for the deeds of a good Samaritan. As everyone moves forward in this case, it is my deep and sincere hope that the lessons from the writings of Julian of Norwich will be observed by all of us, including myself. There are spiritual pains that still require contrition, compassion and a greater love of our Lord. There are also pains that require a greater love of our neighbor.

Chapter 13 --- The Disparity Between Catholic And Secular Governance

*A*s noted several times in this book, this case has been of interest to me because of its seeming difference in religion-based versus faith-based morality. Despite that difference, it is my belief that everyone involved in this case was trying to do their best to fulfill their moral obligations.

Nevertheless, the religion-based procedures as applied in this case seemed to be at odds with faith-based morality.

The question then arises as to what it may have been that led some very good people within the hierarchy of the Catholic Church to overlook the faith-based aspects of the case. Sometimes the greatest strengths of individuals and organizations can also be their weaknesses. Lacking other explanations for some of the actions taken in this case, the issue of governance deserves some exploration.

Most of us who live in this country are well aware of the secular moral issues that divide us. Politicians and members of the news media bombard us with these differences every day.

The governance of our nation is secular. In order to help achieve a high level of secular justice, our government has three branches; executive, legislative and judicial. It was the intent of our founding fathers that those three branches would provide a system of checks and balances so no one branch would become too powerful. When there is too much power in any one of the three branches justice may not be well-served.

The governance of the Catholic Church and most of its religious orders is far different than the secular governance of our nation. In matters of faith and morals, the Catholic Church believes its decisions are guided by the Holy Spirit. It also believes that the Pope is a successor to St. Peter, the first Pope, and thus much power is placed in the Pope and distributed through the Bishops.

Because that governance carries with it the belief of infallibility in certain matters of faith and morals, the need for checks and balances is limited. As Catholics we are the beneficiaries of our Church's governance, because we also believe in the guidance of the Holy Spirit.

In George Weigel's book, "The Courage to be Catholic", he addressed some of the shortcomings of our bishops' governance in dealing with the issue of clerical sexual abuse. At times, one can broaden such shortcomings when it comes to dealing with secular matters within the Church. Its more autocratic form of governance can be of hindrance at times, when it comes to dealing with secular matters.

The Church governance on matters of faith and morals works extremely well with the strong central authority placed within the Vatican. When we believe it is our Pope through whom the Holy Spirit directs us, such governance is easy to accept by faithful people, who wish to observe the commands and wishes of our Lord. It is easy to understand why the Church has now existed for almost two thousand years. It is not subject to the whims of politics in matters of faith and morals.

However, when dealing with secular matters the governance of the Church is not immune from errors. In making rules and procedures of a secular nature, infallibility does not exist. In dealing with the issue of clerical sexual abuse, the Church's policies, rules and procedures continue to evolve. From a governance standpoint the Church's inclination to handle secular matters from a central and more authoritative manner has sometimes worked poorly. Checks and balances in decision making are lacking and too often due process is also lacking. Too frequently the Church's hierarchy serves as prosecutor, judge and jury in matters that do not deal with faith and morals.

This difference in the way the Church handles secular matters versus the way our nation handles such matters causes conflicts. It not only causes conflicts between Church and State, but also causes conflicts between the Church and the people it finds itself often judging.

The recent high profile cases of Father John Corapi and Father Frank Pavone highlight some of these problems. Fathers Corapi and Pavone were beloved by many lay people within the Church. Father Corapi's method of proclaiming the word of God inspired many as did Father Pavone's work in the area of the sanctity of life. The cases of both would have been handled far differently in our secular justice system.

Father Corapi felt it was necessary for him to resign as a priest, because he felt the procedures of the Church made it impossible for him to be judged fairly. As this is being written the case of Father Pavone remains unresolved. Based on news reports, his problem stems from the management of finances.

Church governance may also explain some aspects of this case which deals with APUFRAM and Father Emil Cook. What was too often overlooked is that it also involves the poor children of Honduras. It began with the rape case in Liberia which was committed by a secular, Honduran citizen, who was an employee of APUFRAM, which is a secular foreign organization, albeit with close ties to the Catholic Church.

It is a very questionable matter if a religious Order located in the United States should even have been involved in the case, except that Father Emil Cook was a member of the Order. Even the USCCB acknowledged it had no jurisdiction in the case. Despite that acknowledgement, it circulated the MEMO in December, 2009 which has often been referred to in this book.

Once the religious Order was involved it acknowledged that it was using Church standards and procedures to deal with the case. One of the problems with that approach was that such standards and procedures were intended to be applied in clerical sexual abuse cases which were not involved in this case.

The religious Order then proceeded with the case pursuant to its method of governance. Only they can explain why they chose to insert themselves into a case in Liberia that dealt with a secular crime committed by a secular foreign citizen. Only they can explain why they decided to be the adjudicators of allegations made against secular foreign citizens of Honduras.

It is difficult to understand what the religious Order would have done if it had performed an investigation.

Only they can explain what actions they may have taken if they believed a foreign citizen had been guilty of a crime in Honduras.

Their insertion into this case and their use of the rules and procedures that serve their Order have made this case tremendously complex and one that may never be resolved. It is unfortunate that the memo that harms the children of Honduras, may be operative for a long period of time and given the problems that accompany any attempts at an investigation, an assumption can be made that it may never be revoked.

It is not for me to judge the people involved in this case or the personal motives that may be related to this case. It is my effort to examine the moral aspects of the actions taken in this case.

As stated several times earlier, it is my belief that everyone involved was trying to do their best to deal with a very complex situation. It is also my belief that the way religious orders govern themselves and their members may have added to the complexity of the case.

Despite those beliefs, it is my view that all the parties involved could and should have made a greater effort at understanding one another and doing so in a more peaceful manner. As discussed in Chapter 10 the

Thompsons demonstrated what could be accomplished through working in a more loving and compassionate manner. They found the way of the good Samaritan to be the better path.

Chapter 14 --- The Need For Holiness

This is a book which has been very emotionally and spiritually difficult for me to write. It is difficult because my wife and I have been long-time supporters of the mission work done by Father Emil. We believe his philosophy of God - Study - Work is a good approach. It is disheartening for both of us to know that hundreds of children are needlessly being denied a better life. It is also difficult because it has been necessary to be critical of actions taken by people for whom I have a great deal of respect. I truly believe they were doing their best to perform their duties according to rules prescribed by religion-based morality.

It is also difficult to write this type book, because it has been a constant reminder that the timber in my own eye may be far bigger than the speck in the eyes of those, whose actions I have criticized. It has been a constant reminder that it is difficult to judge ourselves and that we should not judge others. We are humans and as such we do err.

Because of those difficulties this book has gone through numerous unpublished editions by me. There have been many times when I decided against publication. But when those occasions occurred there always seemed to be an internal voice that told me to get back to writing. It kept telling me that if it truly was my belief that the faith-based morality of Jesus cannot be subordinated to secular religion-based rules and procedures then it deserved proclamation and publication.

Jesus took the Pharisees to task because they did not apply their rules and procedures in a merciful, compassionate and loving manner. His message seemed to apply to this case.

From the time He was on earth until the present day Jesus could have re-issued his warnings to every generation. His words of warning to the Pharisees are applicable to each of us. Are we not hypocrites when we know we should love our neighbor as our self but fail to do so? We know his commands but too often fail to think or perform accordingly.

In his letter to the Romans, St. Paul stated it very well, albeit with many words: *What I do, I do not understand. For I do not do what I want, but I do what I hate. Now if I do what I do not want, I concur that the law is good. So now it is no longer I who do it, but sin that dwells within me, that is, in my flesh. The willing is ready at hand, but doing the good is not. For I do not do the good I want, but I*

*do the evil I do not want. Now if I do what I do not want,
it is no longer I who do it but sin that dwells in me. So, then,
I discover the principle that when I want to do right, evil is
at hand. For I take delight in the law of God, in my inner
self. but I see in my members another principle at war with
the law of my mind, taking me captive to the law of sin that
dwells in my members.*

All of us on earth participate in the spiritual struggle St.
Paul describes. To win that struggle we must first seek
that morality, which to the best of our ability, we believe
is what He has taught us. It has frequently been noted
in this book that the highest form of morality is that
which is in accord with the teachings of our Savior, i.e.
faith-based morality. But even after we understand the
morality He wishes us to follow, we must be prepared
to sacrifice the desires of our flesh and mind and act
according to the spiritual wisdom of our soul.

In this case, it is my view, that secular religious rules
were permitted to supersede faith-based morality. The
actions resulting from that, in my opinion, were at the
root of subsequent problems.

Our Lord's wish for all of us is that we act in accord
with His commands. When we do that we follow faith-
based morality. But our Lord asks for even more than
that. Morality defines actions, but we must also work
constantly to increase the fervor of our faith. It is our
soul that must daily yearn for Him. He loves us beyond

our ability to love Him, but He expects us to try and by trying more every day we increase that love of Him.

This case along with too many real clerical sexual abuse cases and the general decline in faith-based morality point out the need for all of us to each and every day increase our love of Him and His commands. Our love of Him needs to go beyond our outward moral actions. It is holiness and love of Him which He desires. Even though people in this case were trying to do their best, it proved that our best is not good enough.

He told us, "You shall love the Lord, your God, with all your heart, with all your soul, and with all your mind. This is the first commandment. The second is like it: You shall love your neighbor as yourself. The WHOLE LAW and the prophets depend on these two commandments".

In these commands there is no need to choose between the need to feed and educate the poor children of Honduras or to put in safeguards for child protection. Both need to be chosen. By their actions some involved in this case do not agree with that viewpoint. I do not understand that assessment.

If we follow His law we should want to do both and we should want to do both as a matter of loving Him. Love conquers all. At the apex of love, evil cannot exist. Heaven knows no evil. The simple fact that this case caused too much anguish is proof that sufficient love of one another was lacking.

Everyone involved in this case, including me, must work harder to love as He loved us. We can again turn to the writings of St. Paul to better understand. *The fruit of the Spirit is love, joy, peace, patience, kindness, generosity, faithfulness, self-control. Against such there is no law.*

As was stated in the Introduction to this book, this is a sad story as regards those poor children of Honduras, whose education has been denied via the suspension of funding to APUFRAM. That may be offset somewhat by the fact that the children who are still cared for by APUFRAM are now living in a safer environment.

But it is also my view that there are no coincidences with our Lord. Things happen for a reason. This case may be a gentle reminder from Him to all of us that we cannot just be obedient to our very good earthly rules and procedures but that we must do so in a holy manner. He wishes for all of us to be forgiving, merciful, compassionate and loving.

That was His message to the Pharisees. That is His message to us.

About The Author

$\mathcal{G}$eorge E Pfautsch spent most of his working life as a financial executive for a major forests products and paper company. His final years at Potlatch Corporation were spent as the Senior Vice-President of Finance and Chief Financial Officer. Following his retirement, he began writing and speaking about the national morality he believes was intended for this nation by the founding fathers of our country. He is the author of five previous books on the subjects of morality, justice and faith. He is the co-author of a book written by Melitta Strandberg which is the true story of her family's quest for freedom before, during and after World War II. He and his wife, Dodi, will celebrate their 50th wedding anniversary during 2012. He has two children and four grandchildren.